To Kathy, Becky, and John, who bring me great joy.
To Susan, for beauty and adventure.
And, in loving memory
of Wilbert Coleman, Lorrie Streyffeler,
and Renate Tesch, whom I miss very much.

Courageous Teaching

Creating a Caring Community in the Classroom

Jim Andersen

For information address:

 Corwin Press, Inc.
2455 Teller Road
Thousand Oaks, California 91320

SAGE Publications Ltd.
6 Bonhill Street
London EC2A 4PU
United Kingdom

SAGE Publications India Pvt. Ltd.
M-32 Market
Greater Kailash I
New Delhi 110 048 India

Printed in the United States of America

Library of Congress Cataloging-in-Publication Data

Andersen, Jim, 1935—
    Courageous teaching: creating a caring community in the classroom
/Jim Andersen.
        p. cm.
    Includes bibliographical references.
    ISBN 0-8039-6239-8 (pb: alk. paper)
    1. Group work in education. 2. Motivation in education.
3. Interpersonal relations. 4. Learning, Psychology of. I. Title.
LB1032.A47 1995
371.3′95—dc20   94-41360

This book is printed on acid-free paper.

95 96 97 98 99 10 9 8 7 6 5 4 3 2 1

Corwin Production Editor: Diane S. Foster

Contents

Preface

I am writing this book to share with others what has become the most exciting and important period of my life, changing from a traditional teacher and school counselor to a facilitative educator. This shift culminated in the creation of a new educational model for working more effectively with students.

My early experiences as a traditional educator left me with a growing awareness that I was having little impact in my school. I came to recognize that I rarely assisted students with their real problems: boredom, anger, shyness, loneliness, confusion, and discouragement.

This awareness prompted me to embark on a professional search to see if I could find a way that would permit me to be of "real" assistance to all students and to work with them in a way that would make school more meaningful for them. I began to integrate concepts from reading and psychological training experiences with an analysis of what was happening during my experimentation in the classroom. This led to a synthesis—the development of a group process conceptual framework and a practical model for facilitating learning.

It shocks me to write that I have been working with group process for more than 25 years. During this period, I studied group process under renowned practitioners. Much as I was influenced by these talented mentors, my "real" teachers have been the thousands of students with whom I have been privileged to work. From young people I have learned the most about the art and science of human relations. Children are more apt than adults to let you know whether your work with them is legitimate. For me, the most challenging grade level for using group process is high school sophomores. When tenth graders refuse to participate in a group process activity, I know this activity still needs some work. And, when I am successful in facilitating group process activities with sophomores, I know these activities will work with any age group.

This book contains (a) a curriculum of sequenced and developmental group process activities designed to make school meaningful for every student, (b) a description of how to become skillful with the art and science of facilitative group process, and (c) information on how to create a caring learning environment in which young people are simultaneously engaged emotionally and intellectually.

The focus is twofold: enabling students to become good persons while they are becoming academically proficient. It is a model for infusing character development into the curriculum whereby every lesson becomes meaningful and purposeful to students.

This book will serve as a guide for courageous educators who want to use group process with students in the classroom. I say "courageous" because, as powerful and effective a tool as group process is, many high school students are initially cautious about participating in group process activities. High school students in particular will wait to see if they can trust the facilitator, and whether the activities are meaningful, before they will openly participate.

The process and activities presented in this book have been tested with thousands of students and educators across the country and will work in every classroom and at every grade level. Only the language and content of some activities may need to be modified for young children. The model's structure and nature are effective for any age.

Each educator holds the potential for learning how to use this program. It is only a matter of courage and practice.

Acknowledgments

Certain mentors have contributed in meaningful ways to my growth as an educator. Foremost among these are Jim Carnevale, Rudolf Dreikurs, Harold Engen, Lacy Hall, Hallock Hoffman, Al Huang, Frederic Hudson, Clay Jenkinson, James Kavanaugh, Rollo May, Ashley Montagu, Carl Rogers, and Renate Tesch.

I am very grateful to Ann Andersen and the students and faculty at Algona High School, where this journey all began. I am particularly appreciative of Elgin Allen, the high school principal who provided the opportunity and support to initiate this work. In addition, several educators lent critical support in the early stages of the program: Ed Meyer, Don and Jane Nettleton, Guy Olson, Dick Palmer, and Dale Teeter.

At the Heartland Area Education Agency, I am especially appreciative of Bill Clark, who employed and empowered me to continue my work with facilitative education, and to Phil Berrie, Joe Millard, and Wayne Rand, who have maintained a sustaining interest in my work. Several of my colleagues have also contributed in meaningful ways, in particular Tom Budnik, Robert Connor, Linda Dale, Barry Metzger, Richard Murphy, Janean Ross, Ed Skowronski, John Thompson, Curt Van Gilder, and Mike Szymczuk.

Over the years I have collaborated with many individuals who have facilitated courses based on this model, including Bruce Anderson, Winston Black, Sandra Bury, Steve Carnahan, Roxanne Caldwell, Roger Evans, Wanda Everage, Jo Fitz, Stephanie Furstenau, Ruth Ann Gaines, Maria Garcia-May, Vicki Goldsmith, Bonnie Graeber, Jim Graeber, Diane Greaves-Crozier, Chuck Greenwood, Don Hall, Margaret Harden, Jim Hollebeek, Tim Huisman, Jackie Hopkins, Susan Imhoff, Julie Johnson, Wayne Jostes, David Leonard, Susan Lewis, Kathy Lucs, Tom Ludwig, Sheilah Manley, Carolyn McCall, Darrel Nordhagen, Sara Otto, Lois Ousley-Edwards, Ezra Rice, RaeGene Robbins, Joan Roberts, Cindy Rohwedder, Johnnie Rothschild, Mary Ann Schmidt, Connie Schnoebelen, Glendora Schuldt, Lois Schultz, Alita Siasoco, Barbara Skjei, Ed Skowronski, Michele Soria-Dunn, Judy Strohbehn, Hance Throckmorton, Judy Tomenga, Jerry Triplett, Mark Weston, Donna Wilkin, David Wilkinson, Granville Williams, Rick Williams, Carmen Winters, and Crys Yaryan.

This manuscript has undergone thoughtful examination by several readers who have helped me to clarify concepts, uncover omissions, and identify the superfluous. In particular I am indebted to Alice Foster, Diane Foster, Victoria Gamber, Vicki Goldsmith, Mark Weston, and Granville Williams for their help.

To all of you, I say thank you.

About the Author

JIM ANDERSEN (Ph.D.) is a nationally recognized specialist in human relations and collaborative education. He serves as a mentor to hundreds of educators and has facilitated seminars on many university campuses in over 20 different states. He works with a wide variety of disciplines, including business, counseling and psychology, education, and health. In addition, he has served as a facilitator for the Education Commission of the States, the National Conference of State Legislatures, the National School Board Association, the Danforth Foundation, and the Texas School Board Association. He has held positions of leadership and distinction in the counseling and education professions. He has served as President and Executive Director of the Iowa Association of Counseling and Development and as President of the Iowa Association of Small Group Workers. He was named "The National High School Counselor of the Year" by the American School Counselor Association. Dana College recognized him with "The Distinguished Alumni Award." The Des Moines Chapter of Phi Delta Kappa presented him with "The Iowa Educator of the Year Award." In 1990 he participated in the (Iowa) Governor's Conference on Education Goals and was a regional participant in the 1991 National Education Goals Panel. He serves as coordinator of the Humanities Program at the

"Heartland Area Education Agency," an intermediate facility serving 7,000 educators in Des Moines and central Iowa. Over 20,000 educators have taken his human relations and collaborative education courses.

Introduction

A New Model

Our most pressing educational problems are human relations problems. They stem from how students relate to one another, themselves, and their environment. Many youth feel alienated, angry, bored, confused, shy, and not loved. An increasing number of students, unable to cope with their feelings of insecurity, escape through avoidance, taking drugs, dropping out of school, or committing suicide. Others have turned to violence and crime. The social, psychological, and economic costs of these unhealthy behaviors are forcing this country to desperately look for solutions.

We can do better. Democracy is at stake because our educational system is failing. It is time to rethink and remake social relations to be an important part of educational reform. Too many students are falling through the cracks because they are not learning to become responsible citizens. The school is our last resort for helping many of these young people.

Educators hold a key position for addressing societal problems. They can help young people become morally and ethically responsible as well as academically proficient. The purpose of this book is to present a comprehensive model that responds to our most pressing social and educational needs. Developed and field-tested in scores of classrooms with hundreds of educators and thousands of students over a period of 20 years, this model is effective in the "real world" of the classroom.

Five strands are woven into this book: (a) democracy, a great idea whose time has come for schools; (b) classrooms as caring communities, creating learning environments that respond to the real needs of students; (c) the art of facilitative process, democratic strategies for successful implementation; (d) an innovative curriculum, sequential and developmental activities that have meaning for the student; and (e) the classroom teacher as change agent, school transformation teacher by teacher and classroom by classroom.

The educational paradigm has changed and the traditional approach to education is now outdated. We need to transform our schools into institutes where students study the art and science of human relations. Schools must adopt practices that help young people become good persons who possess effective problem-solving and human relations skills.

This book shows how to build a caring classroom community where young people are simultaneously engaged emotionally and intellectually. The students are inspired, and an ethical character is developed through activities infused with great ideas.

Every lesson becomes meaningful because each student is engaged in the learning process. Grounded in democratic principles, this model infuses the "New Rs" of *reflection, responsibility, relationships,* and *respect* into the curriculum.

Mastering the Conceptual Framework for Caring Classrooms
A Facilitative Approach to Human Relations

This model was developed in response to educator requests for activities that will stimulate student participation in small group activities. When I began work on this system in the late 1960s, not much was available in the way of group process activities. I combed through books looking for ideas to help create or synthesize an activity. Gradually, I assembled activities into a certain order. In the beginning, the ordering was governed by my perception of the degree of risk the participants would encounter with an activity. I maintained a record of the activities that proved to be successful. Initially, my primary criteria for evaluating activities were the number of students who participated and their apparent degree of enthusiasm for the activity as observed by the teacher.

As I became more adept at selecting and creating activities, student participation increased. I recognized that an important key to my success was the synthesized curricula of activities I was developing. One of my primary insights concerned the certain order into which I was arranging the activities. I started to wonder why this order worked. To find the answer, I began to dissect the curricula by classifying the nature of each

1

activity. I continued to refine the classification process until I had seven categories: caring, sharing (self-disclosure), awareness, respect, faith, self-responsibility, and purposefulness.

The Three Themes

As I continued to read and experiment, three themes emerged that became the basis for this personal growth philosophy. I have identified these themes as (a) the experiential, (b) the developmental, and (c) the transcendental.

The Experiential Theme

The experiential theme is the foundation out of which the other two themes emerge. Unless you are aware of what you are experiencing, there is no opportunity for personal growth or intentional change. Through studying the literature pertaining to this theme, I discovered the characteristics necessary for creating activities that would establish experiential learning environments.

Very few teaching models are concerned with the quality and nature of experience. Most focus on the posture of the teacher and the content of the curriculum. They do not specifically deal with what the student is experiencing during the lesson.

Carl Rogers (1969) was among the first to recognize the significance of the "experience" of the person with whom he was working. He found he was unable to really help someone when he relied solely on intellectual or training procedures. Approaches that rely on knowledge, on training, on the acceptance of something that is taught, are of little use. Real understanding seems to come about only when we are aware of our experience in the relationship.

In experiential learning, there is a quality of personal involvement. The whole person—both feelings and cognitive aspects—is involved in the learning event. It is self-initiated. The learner evaluates the experience and determines whether it is meeting a need or leading in a meaningful direction. To Rogers, the very essence of the experience is *meaning*. When such learning takes place, the element of meaning to the learner is built into the whole experience.

Facilitating learning, then, in this context, comes to include creating conditions in which learners become aware of their experiences and the consequences of their experiences. The learning paradigm becomes one of helping individuals gain access to their personal and interpersonal experiences and to discover the structure and boundaries of these experiences. The learning process, then, is essentially controlled by the learner, not by the facilitator or teacher.

This is a radically different approach to learning, creating learning environments rather than providing specific contents. Traditionally, there is only an emphasis on filling up minds and communicating concepts.

The Developmental Theme

Through participating in experiential activities, students begin to develop and grow. They learn new and important things about themselves, others, and their capacity to become better persons.

Self-acceptance is an important ingredient. The movement toward personal growth comes from the ability to express deep self-acceptance. By learning through our own experiences to accept and to be ourselves, we are taking an important step toward positive change and personal growth. We grow most when we learn to the degree that we are able. Learning, according to Milton Mayeroff (1971), is primarily the re-creation of one's own person through the integration of new experiences and ideas, rather than the mere addition of information and technique.

Each of us has the capacity to discover and discontinue debilitative behavior and to choose behavioral patterns that lead toward full development of our potential. Ultimately, we are responsible for what we become, whether we are conscious of doing so or not, whether we desire to do so or not. To a considerable extent, we can direct and regulate our "becoming process."

The Transcendental Theme

Abraham Maslow (1971) believed the most important concern of the school should be to help young people to become good persons. Through activities that are *experiential* and *developmental* in nature, students can rise above that which they have been and become more of what they might be. This occurs when young people experience activities that are intentional, purposeful, and meaningful.

It is within this transcendental realm that a person sees what might be—a hope for things to come. In this way, the transcendental level is concerned with the awakening and use of superconscious energies that have a regenerative influence on the personality.

To Maslow, it is in this realm that people come to appreciate universally prized values such as love, beauty, and truth more than money, power, and prestige. Through appreciation of the higher values, people rise above (transcend) their capacity for doing evil. Universally prized values provide the way to attain peak experiences, those transient moments of ecstasy.

It is the transcendental processes that lead individuals to attain something beyond themselves. Roberto Assagioli (1965) describes it as striving for a higher goal and thereby acquiring a personality integration at a higher level of development. At this level, a synthesis of rich and idiosyncratic experiences occurs.

The transcendental theme is not substantively different than the experiential and developmental; it includes them. Transcendental processes are experiential and developmental. The experiential theme is the core theme. Unless you "experience," you do not "develop" and "transcend" what you are and thereby become what you might. The themes are interrelated. The experiential theme is also a part of the developmental, and the two are blended with the transcendental. Each alone is insufficient for promoting and sustaining personal growth. It has been my experience that, when combined in a systematic approach, they facilitate a movement toward personal development and the potential for creative living.

The Sequential Stages That Facilitate Personal Growth

Personal growth takes place when the themes are transformed into a series of stages that are systematic and progressive. The integration of growth at the Stage 2 level necessitates having first experienced Stage 1. When the means are provided for students to experience Stage 1, and then to reflect on that experience to develop an understanding of their experience and ultimately to integrate that experience into their person, personal growth takes place.

The experiential theme, which I found to be the core theme, gives birth to what might be—through providing experiences in caring, self-disclosure, and awareness. Cognitive understanding of these stages is insufficient; one must experience them in order to grow.

As you experience yourself and others through caring, self-disclosure, and awareness, you begin to develop self-respect and a desire for becoming self-responsible. Thus the experiential theme is the precondition to the development of self-respect and self-responsibility.

When you develop a sense of self-respect and a desire for being self-responsible, you come to recognize your potential for transcendency. The stages of faith and purposefulness evolve out of and contribute to the theme of transcendentalism. They are the "glue" of the means to intentional living (see Figure 1.1).

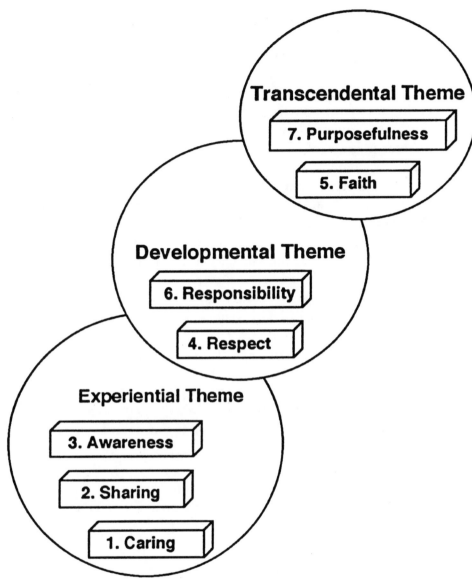

Figure 1.1. The Sequential and Developmental Themes and Stages

Many scholars have valued the stages of personal growth that I have identified and have elaborated on one or more of them in detail. However, none has analyzed the stages that facilitate personal growth as encompassing the seven that I present; nor has any organized them into the order in which I present them. What is unique about this theory is the manner in which I have integrated the stages into a sequential, developmental process. In the third chapter, I will detail the practical application of the stages in this facilitative approach to human relations. At this point, I will enlarge upon the theoretical base of the sequential process.

Stage 1: Caring—The Foundation Stage

Many psychologists have recognized the important position caring holds in facilitating personal growth. However, few have elaborated upon it as thoroughly as Milton Mayeroff (1971), who found that, through caring for certain others, we serve them and in the process live out the meaning of our own lives. In the sense in which we can ever be said to be at home in the world, we are at home not through dominating, or explaining, or teaching, but through caring and being cared for.

To Mayeroff, caring demonstrates faith—faith in oneself and in others. There is hope that the other will grow through my caring. Faith in this context is an expression of a present alive with possibilities. Few things are as encouraging to a person as to recognize that another has faith in him or her. Caring in this capacity is encouraging; you acquire the confidence to drop all pretense.

It has been my experience that, when I demonstrate caring for you, I encourage you, inspire you to have the courage to be yourself. I find that you will be less guarded and more spontaneous in your behavior. Few things are more encouraging than to realize that your growth evokes my admiration and joy because you are profoundly cared for by me. When people experience caring (being deeply understood and appreciated), their defensiveness begins to fade and a willingness to self-disclose emerges. In this way, caring is the precondition to the second stage of the process—self-disclosure.

Stage 2: Sharing
(Self-Disclosure)—The Means to Self-Discovery

I believe that, without self-disclosure, there is little likelihood personal growth will take place. Self-disclosure is the precondition to self-awareness. It includes revealing feelings and thoughts as a means for becoming self-aware. Sidney Jourard (1971) puts it this way: "When a man discloses his experience to another, fully, spontaneously, and honestly, then the mystery that he was decreases enormously" (p. 5).

Jourard's research points strongly to the likelihood that you will disclose yourself, permit yourself to be known, only when you believe those who are with you are of goodwill. Self-disclosure is perceived as risky because it involves letting others see us as we really are.

Recognition of the importance of genuineness and transparency is not new. Sages in every age and culture have urged humanity to move toward authenticity in living. Lao Tsu, Shakespeare, Soren Kierkegaard, and Robert Frost all emphasized the importance of knowing and remaining true to yourself—to that which you really are. Hermann Hesse (1971) expressed it most eloquently for me through urging us to live in accordance with the promptings that come from our true selves and to stop seeking the truth in others: "Don't try to imitate the thinker or ascetic man, but be yourself, try to realize yourself. . . . [W]hat does it mean to realize oneself? . . . [I]t is the highest of all concepts: perfect being" (p. 278).

Why is it so difficult for people to be themselves? I believe that it is primarily a result of alienation. Societal conditions are a contributing factor. Jourard describes our society as alienated, as one in which children do not know their parents. Fathers don't know their children. Husbands and wives are often strangers to one another to an incredible degree.

Jourard (1971) found that self-disclosure is the means whereby a person leaves the state of alienation. The lesson we have learned in psychotherapy is "that no man can come to know himself except as an outcome of disclosing himself to another person" (p. 6). For me, self-disclosure is the precondition to awareness, the third stage in the sequential process that facilitates personal growth.

Stage 3: Awareness—Everything Is Grounded in Awareness

Awareness is the only basis of knowledge and communication (Perls, 1969). As you learn to listen and see with your own eyes and ears, you discover for yourself that which no great teacher could teach you.

When you are able to focus fully and clearly, you increase your capacity to respond. Awareness by itself brings about new experience and leads to new awareness. A basic procedure for gaining increased awareness is to simply express what is being experienced. This emphasis on awareness in action is critical. Only while we are doing it can we become fully aware of who we are and what we do.

Before intentional learning and growth will occur, I believe we need to become aware of three key elements: strengths, needs, and values. Through the uncovering of personal strengths, a sense of "I can-ness" is fostered within us. By the reclamation of our positive past, past success can become the springboard to future success. While we may learn from our failures, recent research clearly supports that we get more in touch with our potential through focusing upon our strengths than from keying in on our flaws.

Dr. Lacy Hall, through the *Achievement Motivation Program* (1972), emphasizes that the discovery of strengths prepares you for uncovering your needs. And, unless you become aware of your needs, you remain obstructed. By becoming aware of needs, you can discover what is meaningful and necessary to life. Through uncovering your needs, you gain the opportunity to fulfill those needs.

Maslow identified the physiological needs and the need for safety as our most basic human needs. Unless they are fulfilled, a person will not be interested in the fulfillment of higher needs. When your health and safety are threatened, your "higher" needs become secondary to the restoration of health and the elimination of danger.

It is unlikely we will recognize our need for love or attempt to find ways to have this need satisfied as long as our survival needs go unfulfilled. Only when the basic needs are satisfied do we discover our need for belongingness and love. To Maslow, love is the precondition to self-esteem. It is difficult for us to recognize our personal worth when our significant others don't demonstrate love for us.

Maslow's hierarchical nature of needs continues with self-esteem being the precondition to the need for knowledge. Why know anything, if you don't like yourself? It seems to me there is no necessity for knowledge if you feel you aren't worth knowing anything. I believe schools need to understand this, if they want to help children learn. A child's need for self-esteem must first be met before the child will show interest in reading, writing, and arithmetic. Interest accompanies the primary need. When a lower hierarchical need is great, that is where the interest will be.

Knowledge is the precondition to the appreciation of beauty. This is a logical explanation for why so few young people visit art galleries, attend the theater, listen to symphonic orchestras; they don't have an interest or appreciation for the fine arts because they don't have the basic knowledge that is essential to their appreciation. Lower, unfulfilled needs are taking precedence in their lives.

The third component of the awareness stage is the identification of personal values. Values are the signposts by which character is developed. Through becoming aware of cherished values, you are better prepared for making choices when faced with alternatives. It is difficult to make choices if you don't have your values sorted out. As you discover the things you value most, it becomes possible for you to choose selectively and thereby not violate your most important values. As Lacy Hall says, we live a life that is most in harmony when we violate least those values we prize most.

Abraham Maslow (1970) encouraged educators to awaken and cultivate universal values in young people. He believed we would have a great flowering of a new civilization if we were to accept as a major educational goal the awakening and fulfillment of the B-values (values of being: truth, goodness, love, beauty, wholeness, aliveness, uniqueness, perfection, completion, justice, playfulness, self-sufficiency, order, simplicity, and so on), which is simply another aspect of self-actualizing. With increased responsibility for our personal lives, and with a rational set of values to guide us in our choices, we could begin to actively change the society in which we live.

Maslow ultimately concluded that these primary values are and should be the far goals of education, as they are and should be the far goals of psychotherapy, child care, marriage, the family, work, and perhaps all other social institutions. Education must be seen as at least partially an effort to produce the good human being, to foster the good life and the good society.

For Maslow, the final and unavoidable conclusion is that education, like all our social institutions, must be concerned with its final values. These are the principles of choice that help us to answer the age-old questions: "What is the good man?" "The good woman?" "What is the good society and what is my obligation to society?" "What is best for my children?" "What is justice?" "Truth?" "Virtue?" "What is my relation to nature, to death, to aging, to pain, to illness?" "How can I live a zestful, enjoyable, meaningful life?" "What is my responsibility to my brothers?" "Who are my brothers?" "What shall I be loyal to?" "What must I be ready for?"

Through facilitating discovery of the B-values, schools have the potential for helping young people uncover their answers to the questions Maslow poses above. And, in the process, they will be assisting students to become good persons.

Unless we clarify these three areas of awareness (strengths, needs, and values), it remains impossible to live a life with purpose and direction. It is through building on our strengths to fulfill our needs without violating our value system that harmony and meaning are brought to life. This is not a general awareness. It is a very specific awareness.

Awareness of these three components, and disciplined self-choice based on this awareness, contributes to the acquisition of self-respect. You need to understand what it is that is unique, special, and "good" about you to develop self-esteem. Otherwise, you have no basis for liking yourself. For me, then, awareness is the precondition to self-respect.

Stage 4: Self-Respect—The Key to Our Potential

Self-respect is generated through the discovery of what is good about your "self" and through experiencing your potential for doing that which is "good." Roberto Assagioli addresses himself to the significance of self-respect and self-love in the following:

> The first love is love for one's self. Mention of this may occasion some surprise, as love directed toward one's self is generally considered to be synonymous with egotism or narcissism. This kind of self-love does of course exist, but it is not the only kind; here, as always, the great complexity and multiplicity of the human being must be taken into account. In the case of self-love, all depends on what we love in ourselves and how we love it. It is truly egotism if we love the egocentric and separate aspects in us, the craving of pleasure, possessions, and domination. But, if we love what is higher and the best in ourselves, what we are essentially, if we love our potentialities for growth, development, creative ability, and communion with others, then this love, devoid of egotism, urges us to live a life of higher quality. This love then

is not an obstacle to loving others in the same way but, rather a powerful means for doing so. (Robert Assagioli. PSYCHOSYNTHESIS, pp. 91-92. Copyright © 1965 by Robert Assagioli. Reprinted by permission of Sterling Lord Literistic, Inc.)

It is evident that Assagioli's position is consistent with Maslow's. Self-respect emerges through personal clarification of the B-values. Self-respect grows from love for that which is "higher and best in ourselves." And the development of self-respect is the precondition to having faith in yourself and your future.

Stage 5: Faith—A Reason for Optimism

In Nazi death camps, Viktor Frankl (1963) found that faith is important because it gives a person strength and a reason to live. As long as faith persists, one doesn't give up. To Alexander Lowen (1972), faith arises and grows out of one's positive personal experiences, which are the source of self-respect. Self-respect increases a person's inner strength. Your faith is an expression of your inherent vitality as a living being just as your vitality is a measure of your faith in life. As long as faith persists, you don't give up your sense of self-respect.

This definition of faith is not to be confused with religious beliefs, for they are not the same. Religious beliefs are bound in dogma and the teachings of others and in this way are more a product of the conscious mind. Lowen defines faith as a product of the heart. You can argue about beliefs and, in the process, confuse a person; you cannot argue with faith.

I believe self-respect nourishes faith. Faith becomes a sustaining power for the person or group sharing a common faith. This becomes evident when we consider some well-known examples. Countless immigrants would never have risked coming to America without having a sustaining and nourishing faith that they could prosper here, nor would the astronauts have risked going to the moon in a spaceship.

In this way, faith is the "living spirit," the source of energy from which people grow in knowledge, understanding, and competency. People possessing deep faith have, throughout the course of history, demonstrated their power to bring about change. As you experience yourself with new and greater capacities, I believe you gain a new faith in yourself and your future. Thus faith is the precondition to responsibility.

Stage 6: Self-Responsibility—The Ability to Respond

Responsibility may be spelled *response-ability*: the ability to respond. Faith gives individuals confidence and assurance that they have the strength, power, or energy to respond—the ability to respond. What is it that holds people back, that blocks them from becoming more than they are? Maslow (1971) believed it is frequently fear of one's own greatness or the evasion of one's destiny or the running away from one's own best talents.

We fear our best as well as our worst, even though in different ways. It is certainly possible for most of us to be greater than we are in actuality. It is certainly true that many of us evade our constitutionally suggested *vocations* (or *calling, destiny, task in life, mission*). So often we run away from the responsibilities dictated (or rather suggested) by nature, by fate, even sometimes by accident, just as Jonah tried—in vain—to run away from his fate.

Assagioli sees humanity as not fixed and immutable but as in a continual state of becoming. To a certain extent, we can direct and regulate our "becoming process." Ultimately, we are responsible for the beneficent or harmful influence we have on others, whether we are conscious of doing so or not, whether we desire to do so or not.

Rudolf Dreikurs (1957) emphasized that we have the capacity not only to react but also to take action. When we are self-conscious, we are in a self-critical state and less able to respond to the situation. When we can unashamedly accept ourselves as we are, we do not limit our ability to respond and we increase our existential being.

Self-responsibility comes with self-determination of what a person wants/needs to know, become, and do. However, you do not become self-responsible unless you also take action for the fulfillment of what you want to know, the kind of person you want to become, and for the things you want to do. Therefore, self-responsibility is a blending of self-determination and self-directed action.

Self-responsibility is the precondition to purposeful living, the ultimate objective of this personal growth process. In reality, all of the previous stages of this sequenced process are the precondition to intentional living.

Stage 7: Purposefulness—The Ultimate Aim

Many young people are living miserable lives without purpose and meaning, as evidenced by the widespread phenomena of juvenile delinquency, rampant crime, terrorism, suicide, boredom, alcoholism, and other forms of drug addiction.

R. D. Laing (1967) believed striving to put meaning in one's life is a primary motivational force. Nietzsche sensed the significance of purposeful living when he wrote: "He who has a why to live can bear almost any how."

The transcendentalists view humanity as free to live with purpose. To Frankl (1963), this freedom must not be confused with arbitrariness. It must be interpreted in terms of responsibleness. Each person is responsible for satisfactorily answering the question: "What will secure meaning in my life?" And meaning is something to be found: It cannot be given to us by others; it must be discovered. It is up to each individual to discover to what, to whom, and for what to be responsible.

Each situation in life presents us with a challenge, with a problem to solve, an opportunity for uncovering the meaning of life. We should not ask what the meaning is; rather, says Frankl (1969), we must recognize it is we who create meaning. In essence, each person is questioned by life, and one can only answer to life by answering for one's own life. You can only respond to life by being responsible if your life is to have meaning. Becoming responsible is the key to purposeful existence.

Intentional living requires a "strong idea," as Freud put it, or a strong ideal to hold on to. Assagioli (1973) has found that ideas of high purpose tend to evoke courage and produce courageous acts. To Rollo May (1969), it is through intentionality and the will to live with purpose that we experience our identity and full potential.

Maslow (1971) found that, without one single exception, people who have made a significant contribution to humanity are involved in a cause outside themselves. They are devoted to something that is very precious to them.

These causes or tasks, which are of great lengths, require steadfastness of purpose. Such was the case with Charles Darwin and the completion of his monumental *Origin of Species*, and with Edison, who tried about 2,000 substances before finding carbon wire for making the electric lightbulb. All were devoted to some task, call, vocation, beloved work. Such people, according to Maslow, tend to identify with their work and to make it a defining characteristic of self. It becomes part of the self. The tasks to which they are dedicated are the embodiment of their intrinsic values. They are not means to an end. Such people are not primarily engaged in their work for money, power, prestige. They are engaged in their work for the value of working. They become their work and their work becomes them. The tasks are loved because they embody values. Ultimately, it is the B-values that are loved rather than the job as such.

We are guided in our search for meaning by our values. Values cannot be taught. They must be uncovered and lived if one is to live with purpose. So it is with meaning; no great teacher or facilitator can give people meaning for their lives. Intentional living must be uncovered by the individual.

Summary

The seven stages and the three themes work together in a systematic and developmental manner, yet are distinguishable entities. Each alone is insufficient for promoting and sustaining personal growth. When combined in this systematic approach, they facilitate a movement toward full humanness, greater creativity, and the realization of more potential.

When you understand the relationship of the themes to the stages that facilitate personal growth, you can select or create activities and exercises that are appropriate for any lesson or situation. You have a standard for evaluating exercises and a rationale for their order of presentation. The themes provide the context within which the very meaning of the process unfolds, giving you a frame of reference.

The themes and stages serve as a guide for selecting and creating activities. They provide a perspective to view occurrences and enable you to proceed with ordering lessons in a meaningful way. The third chapter contains a sequential and developmental curriculum. The second chapter describes the process for facilitating this curriculum. *How* you facilitate is as important as what you facilitate.

Becoming an Effective Facilitator

The Contributions of Carl Rogers

Dr. Rogers developed an innovative approach to working with students over a period of 35 years. His conceptions broadened into what might be called the "facilitative" realm. Unfortunately, few educators have read about Rogers's ideas, methods, and theories of education. Most of his writing is in books whose major focus is on therapy or is found in journals not widely known to educators.

I began to experiment with Rogers's ideas in the classroom and was transformed as an educator by the experience. I observed many positive changes in the young people with whom I worked. Students who had previously been unsuccessful in school began to "bloom."

This chapter describes the nature of the facilitative process and the characteristics of an effective facilitator.

The Facilitative Process

The facilitative model differs considerably from traditional styles of teaching, counseling, and group process. A distinguishing characteristic is the democratic nature in which the facilitator coexists with the participants on an equal social basis.

Students are affected the moment they arrive in the classroom through an arrangement of the furniture that enhances communication and participation. The chairs are placed in a circle so each person is in the front row and no one is seated in an inferior position. In such a setting, everyone has an equal opportunity to learn and contribute to the group. Interpersonal relations and communication are enhanced because facial expressions and eye contact are possible with each participant.

An effective facilitator demonstrates profound respect and sensitivity for each person. The facilitator needs to resist impulses to control, force, direct, manipulate, or push the group—because these behaviors are presumptuous and communicate that the facilitator knows best what others need to know, or how they should be, and what they should do. As the facilitator, it is more appropriate to *invite* participation and to use a facilitative process demonstrating that each of us has sufficient wisdom to figure things out for ourselves as well as the capacity to make a positive contribution at any given moment. The potential for full participation in the facilitative setting is increased because the *action* for learning is controlled by the students and not by the facilitator. The facilitator only controls the process.

The facilitative process flows through the seven sequential and developmental stages of personal growth that have proven to have the capacity to enhance learning and transform lifestyles and relationships. As identified in the preceding chapter, these seven stages are *caring*, building community and a sense of belonging; *sharing*, cultivating active verbal participation; *awareness*, being attentive in the "here and now"; *respect*, for self and others; *faith*, developing confidence and a sense of optimism; *responsibility*, acquiring the ability to take appropriate action; and *purposefulness*, finding meaning, making connections, and engaging in meaningful relationships. A brief review of these stages and their relationship to the process follows.

Caring. I demonstrate caring when I encourage and inspire students to have the courage to be more open, honest, and real. In a caring atmosphere, they are less guarded and more spontaneous in their behavior. Few things are more encouraging to young people than when someone openly demonstrates spontaneous delight and joy over their accomplishment, growth, or understanding. Because learning can be a threatening experience for young people, it is important for them to feel secure enough to risk participation in an educational activity. When students experience caring (being deeply understood and appreciated), their defensiveness begins to fade and a willingness to self-disclose emerges. In this way, caring builds self-confidence and becomes the precondition to the second stage of the process, *self-disclosure.*

Sharing. Sharing is a unique form of self-disclosure and the verbal means by which a person leaves the state of alienation—a major problem in our society and certainly an issue with young people. Sharing is an important activity not only for personal growth and development but for learning as well. I have found in the educational setting that neither the student nor the teacher can be certain if the student really understands the lesson unless the student attempts to explain to another person what is being studied. In this way, sharing is really a form of self-disclosure, which is the precondition to *awareness,* the third stage.

Awareness. Learning equals discovery. Discovery equals awareness. The facilitative approach processes discovery. A basic procedure for gaining increased awareness is simply to express what you're experiencing in the moment. By learning to focus fully and clearly, you increase your capacity to understand and to respond appropriately and effectively. The facilitative approach provides an opportunity for young people to process the structure and boundary of their learning experiences. In this way, they discover their personal strengths, needs, and values. The facilitative process helps students to build on their strengths to fulfill their needs without violating their value system. This specific awareness contributes to the acquisition of *self-respect,* the fourth stage.

Self-Respect. The facilitative approach generates self-respect through helping young people to discover what is good about themselves and through experiencing the capacity for doing and being "good." Self-respect grows from coming to love that which is "higher and best in ourselves." The development of self-respect in an individual is the precondition to having *faith* in oneself and one's future.

Faith. A facilitator is concerned with helping young people to develop inner strength. Faith is an expression of a person's inherent vitality as a living being just as vitality is a measure of a person's faith in life. As long as faith persists, you won't give up your sense of self-respect. With sufficient faith, you believe in yourself and feel secure in your future. Your faith sustains you during times of hardship. When you experience yourself with the capacity and the tendency to move forward to self-actualization, you gain a new faith in yourself and your future. In this way, faith is the precondition to *self-responsibility*.

Self-Responsibility. Faith gives you confidence and assurance that you have the strength, power, and energy to respond—the ability to respond. Self-responsibility is a blending of self-determination and self-directed action. You do not become self-responsible unless you take action for the fulfillment of what you want to do, what you want to know, and what you want to become. Meaningful or intentional living is not possible unless you first take responsibility for your own life. The facilitative approach provides appropriate opportunities for young people to assume increasing levels of responsibility.

Purposefulness. To Rollo May (1969), it is through intentionality and the will to live with purpose that you experience self-actualization and your identity. Maslow found self-actualizing people are, without one single exception, involved in a cause outside themselves. They are devoted to something that is very precious to them. The facilitative approach attempts to help young people cultivate ideas of high purpose that will evoke courageous and worthwhile acts.

The seven stages work together in a systematic and developmental manner, yet are distinguishable entities. It has been my experience that each alone is insufficient for promoting and sustaining personal growth and understanding. When combined in this systematic approach, they facilitate a movement toward full humanness and the potential for creative and purposeful living.

Once you understand the relationship between the stages, you can create or select activities and exercises that facilitate personal growth and learning. You have a standard for evaluating learning activities and a rationale for their order of presentation. These seven stages give you a frame of reference and provide the context within which the very meaning of the facilitative process unfolds.

The Responsibilities of the Facilitator

To be effective, the facilitator must become the facilitative process. If the facilitator tries to *do* the process or to *do* the activity, it becomes mechanistic. To become congruent with the process, the facilitator must become completely knowledgeable of the facilitative process.

To be successful as a facilitator, you must become an artist who cultivates purposeful action through processing discoveries, observations, and perceptions. The art lies in arranging the learning activities and questions in a respectful manner so that every student has the potential to contribute the next important step or question. The facilitator draws out the best each participant has to offer. Through creating a conducive learning environment, the facilitator assists students with becoming more aware, responsible, and competent.

As the facilitator, it is important to refrain from getting up on a "soap-box" to manipulate or sway the students in any manner. Statements of opinion and pronouncements of belief by the facilitator serve to polarize and to create dissension. It is debilitating to the process when the facilitator advances a personal agenda. Learning and participation are enhanced when the facilitator remains a neutral party in the process.

The facilitator does not induce anyone to participate. Instead, an *invitation* to participate is extended to group members. The facilitator endeavors to make each activity a valued experience for every participant. Therefore, no activity is consciously selected that has the potential for providing a negative experience.

While working with the group, the facilitator avoids using "why" questions because they have the potential for getting the group bogged down in it's own history. "What" and "how" questions are the means to effective action because they keep the process grounded in the "present," which is the only place creative action is possible. You can't change history. Change is only possible in the present. Therefore, "why" questions are only used 10% to 15% of the time in a facilitative classroom.

It is the facilitator's responsibility to provide the group feedback on what is transpiring (by speaking to the obvious—that which can be clearly seen). Feedback demonstrates to the person who has spoken that you not only heard the words but also understand the meaning. Using an active listening process, the facilitator routinely provides immediate feedback to each participant as he or she makes a contribution to the group. For example:

Student: I don't know why we have so much homework. I don't have much time to do what I want to do.

Facilitator: You're frustrated because school work seems to consume so much of your time.

Feedback is provided to make certain everyone understands what is being expressed. At the same time, the facilitator refrains from rendering personal judgments or providing interpretations, because this robs the students of the opportunity to draw their own conclusions or to develop critical thinking skills.

Within the facilitative process, the participants are free to confront themselves and to internally process their own feelings and thoughts. When treated in a facilitative manner, the students are less defensive and are more likely to become open and aware of how things are with themselves and with the group. This occurs because the facilitator does not express anger to any participant. Anger may be directed at misbehavior, but never personally at students because it always has a negative impact on young people.

The facilitative process is designed to limit discussion and to encourage *sharing*. Too often, discussion leads to intellectualizing and entrapment in logic, which causes students to be defensive. Discussion then becomes a negative experience and causes people to become argumentative or to cease participation.

Sharing is a positive alternative to discussion. Sharing is a process that encourages young people to state what they have to say without having to defend or to attack someone else's position. When you share rather than discuss, you demonstrate that you have no need to manipulate or control others. This establishes respect and allows the participants to uncover for themselves what is being expressed because no one is preoccupied with defending or proving a point when using the sharing approach. You merely place what you have to say on the "table" from which others may partake, if they wish, without making any effort to force-feed acceptance or understanding. Sharing is respectful because it implies that people have the wisdom to uncover the nature and the quality of what has been expressed without having to have it explained to them. The sharing format allows group members to learn and to participate in their own time and way.

This does not mean that discussion is never used in a facilitative group. There are times when discussion is appropriate. However, discussion should be limited to approximately 10% percent of the time and sharing encouraged 90% of the time. Limiting discussion is an art, and the facilitator must become skillful at respectfully curbing discussion through using process statements, such as the following: "Did anyone notice anything? Any surprises or discoveries? What did you become aware of?" Interventions such as these serve to move the conversation beyond polarizing statements or questions.

Who Should Become a Group Process Facilitator?

Just as every student will not initially take to participation in group process activities, so it is with educators. Some educators may never prove to be successful with group process.

Consequently, no educator should be forced to facilitate groups. When this is done, the results are typically disastrous. Creating environments in which discouraged students may participate in group process activities can be challenging enough without trying to do it with a teacher or counselor who doesn't want to use this methodology.

The ideal way is to start with a small core of educators who are enthusiastic about the concept and willing to put in the time for becoming prepared to facilitate an activity.

It is important for group process facilitators to gather together and try out on one another the activities they want to facilitate with young people. School counselors may be of much assistance to anyone seeking facilitative group process skills. Through participation in ongoing in-service sessions with a counselor, educators may gain confidence and skill. Furthermore, the counselor may be instrumental in discovering why some activities are not working and how to make appropriate adjustments. By taking turns at facilitating the activities with one another prior to working with students, educators can acquire valuable experience and understanding in the art and science of group process. It is difficult to be successful with group process unless one has received assistance from a competent mentor.

Characteristics That Enhance Facilitator Effectiveness

When the facilitator cultivates the acquisition of certain personal characteristics, the participants more readily recognize their capacity for understanding and effectively managing their own affairs.

Authenticity. The first and foremost characteristic is *authenticity*, which includes honesty, genuineness, transparency, presence, and congruence. To be authentic as a facilitator, it is important to be aware of your own feelings so that you do not present an outward facade of one attitude while actually holding a different one. It means that, as the facilitator, you must be transparent—openly expressing your own feelings and attitudes that are flowing at the moment.

Sometimes students behave in a manner that makes the facilitator angry. When this occurs, the facilitator must be authentic with the group, yet not respond in a manner that is disrespectful. To do this, the facilitator needs to speak to the behavior rather than to personally attack a student. For example, the facilitator might say: "I am angry and frustrated when you misbehave in this group because it makes it difficult for everyone else to participate in this activity."

The intent is to be honest with students without making them defensive through a personal attack. People can handle direct confrontation on their behavior; they do not respond well to attacks on their person.

Nonjudgmental. The second condition, essential to the relationship, is for the facilitator to *nonjudgmentally accept each person as a social equal.* This means clearly demonstrating acceptance, affirmation, compassion, and unconditional positive regard for everyone. The facilitative approach requires that the facilitator actively encourage personal expression of feelings and thoughts. You don't have to like what is being expressed—but it is necessary to unconditionally accept the worth of the person who expresses the opinion.

Attentiveness. The third aspect of the facilitative relationship is *attentiveness.* This means that the facilitator must become very observant, noticing every detail communicated. Sometimes the most significant part of the communication is intonation, or it might be body language. Attentiveness leads to conscious awareness, which means you really see and hear what is being expressed and you understand what it means.

Acceptance means very little unless it involves mindful understanding. To really understand someone requires great concentration. It is important to be very observant so you can see how things are with another person. Then as an educator you can grasp what it must be like to be a student in your classroom. When students feel profoundly understood, they become willing to explore the unknown, the confusing, and the frightening. This quality of understanding brings freedom to the relationship, which is essential for learning and personal growth.

In addition to authenticity, nonjudgmentalness, and conscious awareness, it is helpful when the facilitator consciously cultivates the following personal characteristics.

Caring. Caring seems to hold the central position in the facilitative process. Profound caring can permeate an entire group. It becomes an extension of yourself that transcends and becomes something even greater than you. In caring for other people, you experience them as having the potentialities and the need to grow.

Honesty. Intellectual approaches and training procedures alone are seldom effective in helping people to learn, solve problems, or grow. People learn best from educators who are real, authentic, and present. The characteristics of openness and honesty make the facilitator more approachable.

Courage. If you have the *courage* to be yourself—even when you think you are unacceptable—you'll be a good facilitator. Real courage begins with *humility*—being open to learn from any source or person as well as from your own mistakes.

Patience. Patience conveys kindness because you allow students time, space, and the opportunity to learn in their own way, even when this means playfulness, confusion, and slippery behavior. It is important to be patient with yourself as well as with others.

Tolerance. You are arrogant when you choose to see people as you perceive they should be rather than as they are. Tolerance allows people to present themselves without display, concealment, and indirection. When you are tolerant, you allow others to change in their own time and way.

Faith. When you demonstrate faith in yourself and others, you are facilitative. Faith in this context is an expression of a present alive with possibilities. Few things are more encouraging than to discover that someone has faith in you.

Trust. Trusting involves letting go and demonstrates confidence in an individual's ability to learn from mistakes and to make good decisions. A feeling of security accompanies trust.

With the facilitative approach, *how* you are with students is more important than *what* you do with them. It is more important for educators to work on themselves than to try and change students. The more the teacher becomes a better person as the facilitator, the better persons the students become. When the educator is the "first" student in the classroom, the learning atmosphere becomes stimulating and alive with possibilities. Growth and constructive development are enhanced because the educator is also a growing, learning, maturing person.

The Facilitator as Participant

The group setting is not an appropriate place for the facilitator to lay personal beliefs and value judgments on students. It is not the place for a lecture. Rather, the facilitator should participate in each activity as a full person, openly and honestly communicating with students to the degree called for by the activity.

It is counterproductive when the facilitator advises individuals or the group on how to solve their problems. When this occurs, it tends to dull the group. Likewise, the facilitator should avoid making judgments or broad, sweeping pronouncements.

The facilitator should not "come off" as the self-appointed protector of individuals in the group. Cushioning often spoils the experience for a student. The facilitator should intervene only when disrespectful behavior occurs. The participants should be provided an opportunity to express the full range of their being to the group and to experience the group's reaction.

Effective Responses to Student Misbehavior

Students appreciate the option of not having to be an active participant. When young people discover they are not going to be forced to participate, they frequently choose to become active participants. It's human nature, when encountering force or manipulation, to remain inactive or to assume a defensive role.

At the same time, it is important for the facilitator to continue to invite every student to participate and to demonstrate the belief that each student will be a participant. In this way, students find they are always welcome—but that they can come in on their own terms.

With disruptive or openly antagonistic students, the best policy for the facilitator is to remain respectful, but firm. Disruptive behavior and "put-downs" cannot be tolerated because they interfere with, or discourage, students who want to participate. Consequently, the facilitator needs to determine beforehand which options are available as logical consequences for misbehaving students. When the consequences for misbehavior are fair and administered in a respectful manner, young people learn much about responsible citizenship. An excellent source regarding logical consequences is Rudolf Dreikurs and Loren Grey's (1968) *A New Approach to Discipline: Logical Consequences.*

The rewards of active participation in facilitative group process are so great that, once students actively partake of the experience, they are reluctant to engage in misbehavior. Nearly every student can be won over with respect, kindness, and firmness.

Becoming responsible includes being regular in attendance for group sessions. When students are absent or late, there is a negative impact on the dynamics of the group.

Paradoxically, the addition of a new student does not destroy the integrity of the group. The group can tolerate a new participant much more easily than it can withstand sporadic attendance. And the group setting provides a wonderful opportunity for new students to become acquainted and to feel at home in their new school.

Implementing a Curriculum
for a Caring Classroom

This group process approach allows individuals to experience "who they are" and then to re-create themselves as they "want to be." The emphasis is on self-discovery of what constitutes being a "good person" and the development of self-sufficiency and willpower for the actualization of potential.

Through a facilitative approach, the program provides conditions that support the establishment of "community" and promotes healthy interpersonal relations. The participants acquire interpersonal competence through their "community" interexperience. The process is synergetic; that is, it arranges relationships so that one person's advantage is another person's advantage. Thus the participants experience dependence and independence and find that they need not be blocked in either. The participants become aware of their own experiences and the consequences of these experiences. Each individual gains access to personal and interpersonal experiences and learns the structure and boundaries of those experiences. The *facilitative approach* provides the opportunity for the group to experience the freedom and value of interdependence.

There are many group process programs and activities available. Few have demonstrated ongoing effectiveness. What makes this model unique and successful is the developmental sequence that is incorporated. The process is experienced by the participants through a curriculum of activities that stimulate progressive stages of personal growth leading to a greater realization of one's own potential.

The curriculum of sequenced, developmental activities is based on three psychological themes: (a) experiential, (b) developmental, and (c) transcendental. The group systematically passes through sequenced stages of experiences designed to facilitate (a) caring, (b) self-disclosure, (c) awareness of self and others, (d) self-respect, (e) faith, (f) self-responsibility, and (g) purposefulness. The sequenced stages emerge from the three themes that are interlaced and are also sequential.

The experiential theme is the foundation theme. Unless you "experience," you do not "develop" and "transcend" what you are and thereby become what you might. In essence, the experiential theme gives birth to what might be, through providing experiences in caring, self-disclosure, and awareness. Cognitive understanding of these stages is insufficient. A person must experience them in order to grow.

As you experience yourself through caring, self-disclosure, and awareness, you begin to "develop" self-respect and a desire for becoming self-responsible. Consequently, the "experiential" theme is the precondition to the "development" of self-respect and self-responsibility.

With a sense of self-respect and a desire for being self-responsible, you come to recognize your potential for "transcendency." The stages of faith and purposefulness evolve out of and contribute to the theme of transcendentalism. They are the glue of, and the means to, intentional living.

The themes are interrelated in that the experiential theme is also a part of the developmental and the two are blended with the transcendental. In this way, the stages and themes work together in a systematic and developmental manner yet are separate entities. Each alone is insufficient for promoting and sustaining personal growth. When combined in a systematic approach, they facilitate a movement toward full humanness and the potential for creative living.

This conceptual framework provides the basis for selecting and evaluating activities for use in the program. Because the themes relate to certain stages of growth, a rationale exists for their order of presentation.

Implementing the Model

Techniques and Methods for Group Facilitation

This system is unique in that the learning process is controlled by the learner and not by the group facilitator. Consequently, the group facilitator is not a "leader" in an autocratic sense—teaching, advising, or directing the group. The facilitator is facilitating a process that allows for self-discovery. The facilitator is helping students to grow. The facilitator experiences the participants' development as being bound up with her own sense of well-being. The facilitator, as a catalyst, feels needed by the group for their personal growth, learning, and understanding. Therefore, the facilitator responds affirmatively, with devotion, to individual needs and is guided by the participants' direction for growth.

The activities are typically experienced with the participants sitting in a circle. The process works most effectively when there are at least 8 participants. The ideal group size is 16. This phenomenon has vast implications for reducing class size. Because learning is typically a group experience, it makes a big difference if there are too many or too few students in the group.

Some activities take more time than is available in the period. When this occurs, the facilitator reminds the group that this is how life is, and we'll just have to pick up next time where we've left off today.

Only a few rules govern this process, but each rule is extremely important. No one should be forced to participate, but everyone should be *invited* to join the group. Only one person should speak at a time and the facilitator endeavors to respectfully enforce this rule. The activities are presented in such a manner that the participants share with each other rather than discuss. Discussion has a tendency to become a cognitive exercise through which the participants appear impressive while trapping one another in logic. When this happens, people are less willing to risk participation in an activity.

The facilitator is responsible for introducing activities and for helping with uncovering what the participants are experiencing. This is accomplished through asking process questions that are facilitative in nature. When an activity is completed, the facilitator refrains from asking questions like this one: "What have you learned from this activity?" That question reduces the experience to what the facilitator or a few individuals believe was to have been learned. Instead, the facilitator encourages ongoing individual exploration through asking facilitative questions such as these: "Did anyone notice anything?" "Did you discover anything?" "Were you surprised by anything?" Questions of this nature promote ongoing discovery.

In essence, the facilitator invites the participants to discover (a) the kind of persons they are and the kind of persons they are capable of becoming; (b) what they know, need to know, and would like to know more about; and (c) what they are doing, what is worth doing, and what they would like to be doing more frequently. No one has the right to take this responsibility away from us, nor is anyone in a better position than we are to determine answers to these questions.

Starting a Group

When initiating a group, students need to understand that the facilitator will be a full participant and not someone who is doing something to or for the participants. The potential for student participation increases with a proper introduction to group process. An example of how one might open a group follows:

"We're about to begin using an approach that is commonly called group process. You will see me as a full participant—something like being the 'first' student in this class—because there is a lot that I can learn from working with you in this capacity."

"We will be working on becoming more aware of ourselves and others. When we are unaware, we don't deal very effectively with our lives. We need to become more aware of our personal environment to effectively use our power for dealing with situations. So, cultivating awareness will be a very important part of our work together."

"Group process experiences are an opportunity to become more open and honest with one another. People are often afraid to be open and honest in their conversations. Honesty requires courage, and we often sense the risk is too great to be genuine in our relationships with others."

"Toward this end, I'm going to try and help you acquire more self-confidence so it will be easier to be open and honest. As you acquire more self-confidence, you will discover that your self-concept is also improving. Too many people in our society have a low self-image. They don't think they are very good, or that they have much to say. So, they keep most of their personal lives locked up inside of themselves."

"We're going to try to deal with this issue. I believe we can improve our self-concept as we increase our capacity for awareness and honesty."

"To be successful, we need to focus on two kinds of behavior: (1) feedback, which is indicating that we understand what someone is saying or doing, and (2) self-disclosure, which involves paying attention to what we are thinking and feeling, and then sharing this information with individuals with whom we feel comfortable."

"Your participation in group process activities will always be by invitation. This means you are in charge of whether you will participate and the degree to which you will participate. You always have the option of not actively participating. On the other hand, you must always be respectful of others who want to participate."

"A few rules will govern our work together. First, we will usually sit in a circle when the whole group is involved in an activity. Only one person may speak at a time. Personal information must remain confidential. Not only will we not talk about what others express here, we will not talk about anyone who is not present. To do so is gossiping and gossiping is disrespectful."

"As we begin, I want to share a feeling. I have a sense of anticipation, partly because I don't know exactly what's going to happen. This makes it kind of exciting and also a bit frightening—so I'm also somewhat anxious. But, I'm convinced that something good will happen. I'm especially enthusiastic about getting to know you better."

"So, let's get started with an activity related to one of the things I've been talking about—an exercise designed to help us build a sense of community through which we can really get to know one another."

Activities Demonstrating the Sequential Process

Through a systematically prepared curriculum, the group passes through seven sequenced stages of experiences designed to facilitate caring, self-disclosure, awareness, self-respect, faith, self-responsibility, and purposefulness. The progressive nature of the sequenced curriculum is demonstrated in the selected activities that follow in this chapter.

Stage 1: Caring

Caring Is the Precondition to Self-Disclosure

Caring is the foundational stage for building a sense of community with any group. Not only should the activity be caring in nature, it is essential that the group facilitator clearly demonstrate caring for each member of the group. Moreover, this caring must be more than a verbal expression of "I care for you." There are a number of explicit ways in which the facilitator can demonstrate caring deeply. The best approach is when the facilitator clearly demonstrates an understanding of what is being expressed. This involves communicating an awareness of feelings, thoughts, and behavior. It is a precious experience whenever someone demonstrates that he or she understands you.

When a group meets for the first time, most of the participants are somewhat anxious about how things will go. Until people become acquainted with one another and familiar with what is expected of them, they remain wary. All of us, but students in particular, are concerned about losing status. Consequently, it is important that the facilitator begin with activities in which there are no "right" or "wrong" answers and in which the participants don't even have to speak. They only have to raise their hands or show what they have written on paper to communicate with others.

The following are a series of activities designed to facilitate caring and the initiation of a sense of community. They are presented in a sequential and developmental manner.

Caring No. 1—Forced choice: Cross-country vacation. (The following supplies are needed: paper and pencils.) Each participant is invited to choose between alternatives found in the seven different categories pertaining to a cross-country vacation. Which activity would they most prefer? Should some participants not care for any of the alternatives, they may be encouraged to choose the options they find least offensive. As the facilitator reveals the alternatives, category by category, the participants select an option from each of the seven categories and record their choices on a sheet of paper. When all seven categories have been covered, the facilitator invites the participants to move about the group, as if they were in a social setting, comparing lists. Their task is to find individuals with an identical or a completely different list of choices.

A. Mode of travel preferred:
  (1) car   (2) train
  (3) plane   (4) motorcycle
B. Preferred city to visit first:
  (1) Minneapolis   (2) New York City
  (3) New Orleans   (4) San Francisco
C. Preferred national park:
  (1) Everglades   (2) Grand Canyon
  (3) Yellowstone   (4) Yosemite
D. Preferred activity:
  (1) deep-sea fishing   (2) backpacking
  (3) sailing   (4) skiing
E. Type of entertainment:
  (1) comedy   (2) magic show
  (3) musical   (4) drama
F. Preferred attraction:
  (1) Disneyland   (2) Statue of Liberty
  (3) Space Needle   (4) The French Quarter
G. Preferred fruit:
  (1) apple   (2) grapes
  (3) peaches   (4) oranges

After the participants have received sufficient time to compare lists, the facilitator processes the activity through asking if anyone noticed anything or found something surprising or interesting. In this way, awareness and discovery are facilitated.

SOURCE: Andersen. *Courageous Teaching.* © 1995 Corwin Press, Inc. Reprinted with permission.

Option 1a—Forced choice: Cultural awareness tour. (The following supplies are needed: paper and pencils.) The facilitator invites the group to take a cultural awareness tour. Each participant receives the opportunity to choose between alternatives on seven different categories pertaining to the tour. Even though the participants may not care for any of the alternatives, they are encouraged to choose one they find least offensive. The categories are as follows:

A. City of choice:
- (1) Peking
- (2) Paris
- (3) Pretoria
- (4) Pago Pago

B. Mountain:
- (1) Mt. Fuji
- (2) Mt. Kilimanjaro
- (3) Mt. Everest
- (4) Mt. Ararat

C. Sea:
- (1) Mediterranean
- (2) Yellow
- (3) Baltic
- (4) Red

D. Architectural wonder:
- (1) Taj Mahal
- (2) Pyramids
- (3) Great Wall
- (4) Machu Picchu

E. River:
- (1) Congo
- (2) Amazon
- (3) Yangtze
- (4) Ganges

F. Natural phenomenon:
- (1) Amazon rainforest
- (2) Victoria Falls
- (3) Kenyan jungle
- (4) Dead Sea

G. Deserts:
- (1) Great Sandy
- (2) Gobi
- (3) Kalahari
- (4) Sahara

As the facilitator reveals the categories and alternatives, the participants select alternatives from each of the seven categories and record their choices on a sheet of paper.

When all seven have been covered, the facilitator invites the participants to write their names on their sheets of paper and then to move about the group comparing lists. They are encouraged to uncover anyone who has an identical or completely different list.

After the participants have completed the comparison process, the facilitator asks the group what they may have noticed, discovered, or found surprising.

Option 1b—Forced choice: School experiences. (The following supplies are needed: paper and pencils.) The participants are invited to choose among alternatives pertaining to their school experience. In which activity would they most enjoy participating?

A. Art
   1. Paint with watercolors
   2. Form a vase on the potter's wheel
   3. Sculpt a wood carving
   4. Design jewelry

B. Science
   1. Conduct experiments with electricity
   2. Study exotic plants
   3. Conduct behavioral experiments with white rats
   4. Build a telescope and study the stars

C. Composition
   1. Write an essay
   2. Write a poem
   3. Write a short play
   4. Write a short story

D. Mathematics
   1. Keep track of batting averages
   2. Determine the pitch of a roof
   3. Work with complicated formulas
   4. Balance a checking account

E. Fine arts
   1. Sing a solo
   2. Perform the lead role in the school play
   3. Play a string instrument
   4. Dance with a ballet troupe

F. Social studies
   1. Manage a stock portfolio
   2. Read about the Peloponnesian Wars
   3. Participate in a debate on the Civil War
   4. Report on a current event

G. Extracurricular
   1. Serve as a student body officer
   2. Serve as editor of the school newspaper
   3. Play on the basketball team
   4. Play in a band

SOURCE: Andersen. *Courageous Teaching.* © 1995 Corwin Press, Inc. Reprinted with permission.

Find someone who. . .				
has designed or created jewelry.	has taken a woodworking class in school.	has taken ballet lessons.	has dissected a frog.	had an aquarium.
has collected butterflies.	had a poem, essay, or short story published in a school paper.	has studied a foreign language.	has performed in a piano recital.	has sung a solo in a program or concert.
has participated in a school play.	has played on a basketball team.	Please write your name here:	has visited a foreign country.	has served as a class officer.
has attended school in a different state.	plays a woodwind instrument.	has worked on a farm.	has been a cheerleader.	plays the guitar.
has held a part-time job.	enjoys using a computer.	has painted his or her own room.	knows how to play chess.	likes to cook.

Figure 3.1.

SOURCE: Andersen. *Courageous Teaching.* © 1995 Corwin Press, Inc. Reprinted with permission.

Caring No. 2—Find someone who . . . (The following supplies are needed: The worksheet [Figure 3.1] and pencils.) The participants receive the "Find Someone Who . . ." worksheet and are invited to move about the room asking the other participants if they have accomplished any of the activities identified on the form. Those who have had any of the experiences called for may sign their names in the box for the corresponding item. No participant should sign more than two items on anyone's worksheet.

After a sufficient time for completing the activity, the facilitator processes the participants' experiences with them by inviting them to sit in a circle and to share anything they may have noticed or found interesting or surprising.

Caring No. 3—How many of you . . .? The facilitator invites the participants to sit in a circle. This is a nonverbal activity. A list of statements are read to the group and, after each statement, the participants are provided an opportunity to indicate whether or not the statement is true for them by raising their hands. The following are examples of statements:

How many of you . . .

A. like to work with your hands?

B. use Crest toothpaste?

C. play a musical instrument?

D. publicly show affection?

E. would like to drive a sports car?

F. read more than 12 books a year?

G. would rather eat out than at home?

H. like classical music?

I. read the comics daily?

J. regularly get physical exercise?

K. have a good friend of another race?

L. regularly read poetry?

M. sing in the shower?

N. are selective in your diet?

O. play golf?

P. would like to visit Africa?

Q. know how to sail a boat?

R. mow your own lawn?

S. like to use the computer?

T. like to travel?

U. like to whistle?

V. would like to live overseas?

W. have ever been on crutches?

X. enjoy Chinese food?

Y. have climbed a mountain?

Z. like to dance?

Caring Option 3a—Are you someone who believes we will soon . . .?
(Use "Caring No. 3" directions.)

Are you someone who believes we will soon . . .

A. be greeted at airports by robots who will perform security tasks and handle baggage?

B. be wearing high-function and high-fashion computers?

C. have a serious U.S. recession before the year 2000?

D. carry smart cards that contain large amounts of personal information?

E. have many socially responsible businesses like "Ben & Jerry's Ice Cream, Inc."?

F. have court cases decided by artificial intelligence through telecommunication to eliminate personal appearances?

G. be able to carry universal translators capable of instantly translating speech from one language into another?

H. have twice as many older Americans as teenagers?

I. have a return of apprenticeships due to the rising cost of a college education?

J. be using virtual reality and computer simulation as a major element of education?

K. have a major increase of tropical diseases and skin cancers due to the "greenhouse effect"? (The World Future Society predicts all will occur; see Cornish, 1992.)

Caring Option 3b—Are you someone who can match the metaphor with the city? (Use "Caring No. 3" directions.)

A. "The shot heard round the world" (Boston)

B. "The birthplace of democracy" (Philadelphia)

C. "The Big Apple" (New York)

D. "The Big Easy" (New Orleans)

E. "The Entertainment Capitol" (Las Vegas)

F. "The Golden Gate" (San Francisco)

G. "The Industrial Giant" (Chicago)

H. "The Gateway to the West" (St. Louis)

I. "The Mile High City" (Denver)

J. "The Capitol of Country Music" (Nashville)

K. "The City of Roses" (Portland)

Caring No. 4—My favorite . . . (The following supplies are needed: paper and pencils.) The facilitator randomly pairs up the participants and invites them to sit down, facing one another. The participants identify "a favorite" response for each of seven different categories listed below and record their choices on paper. The categories are as follows:

1. A favorite natural setting
2. A favorite musical performer and piece of music
3. A favorite activity
4. A favorite book
5. A favorite form of physical activity
6. A favorite city
7. A favorite meal

The facilitator invites someone in each of the pairs to volunteer. The volunteers go first, sharing what they identified as favorites. Two minutes are provided. The volunteers do all of the talking while their partners just listen.

When the 2 minutes have expired, the facilitator invites those who were listening to demonstrate the degree to which they understood what their partners were saying by phrasing the feedback in their own words. One minute is provided for the feedback. Then the participants switch roles and the process is repeated. The activity is concluded with the facilitator processing insights and discoveries made by individual group members.

Optional "favorite" topics:

A. Painting (picture or statue)
B. Movie
C. Car
D. Personal possession
E. Actor
F. Sport
G. Hope or dream

These are nonthreatening topics and the participants tend to like the challenge of remembering all of the data that have been shared. These activities provide a warm, caring atmosphere and set the stage for succeeding experiences. Through sharing meaningful personal information, the participants rapidly get to know one another and become more comfortable working together.

Through making a sincere effort to care for individual group members, the facilitator comes to know many things, such as individual strengths, needs, and values, as they emerge among members of the group. And, along with the group, the facilitator learns how to respond to him- or herself and to others. The facilitator becomes familiar with appropriate and inappropriate behavior. Facilitative group process essentially creates a human laboratory for self-knowledge and understanding.

Patience is another characteristic cultivated through caring group process activities. As educators, we cannot push the growth of students any more than we can push the growth of a tree or an animal. We must be willing to allow students time, space, and the opportunity to learn in their own way—even when this means playfulness, confusion, and slippery behavior. And we must be patient with ourselves as well as with our students.

If you can tolerate yourself as you are, you can also tolerate others as they are. Self-tolerance goes a long way toward overcoming pretentiousness. It means being able to present yourself without display, concealment, and indirection. The tolerant facilitator allows others to change in their own time and way.

Every activity facilitated in this program should be presented with care and respect. The manner in which the activity is facilitated is more important than the activity itself. The behavior of the facilitator makes or breaks the process for the group. A superb curriculum of activities is rendered ineffective with an uncaring, disrespectful facilitator. It is critical for group development that the facilitator manifest the qualities of the program and function at a high level of facilitative skill.

When the group is not pushed to participate, and the facilitator functions in a caring manner, everyone will choose to participate. With some students it may take more time, which is precisely why patience is important in the caring process. When the students are ready to participate, they will. But, first, they have to feel it is safe.

When group participants experience caring, a sense of community begins to build within the group. This community feeling is evidenced by an increasing willingness on the part of the participants to let down their defenses and to risk letting others get to know them in terms of what they think and feel. In this way, caring is the precondition to self-disclosure, for there is no self-disclosure without participation.

Stage 2: Sharing/Self-Disclosure

Self-Disclosure Is the Precondition to Self-Awareness

Without self-disclosure, there is little likelihood that learning or personal growth will take place. People remain alienated, from themselves and others, until they self-disclose. Self-disclosure is the process whereby we leave the state of alienation and move toward realizing more of our potential. This curriculum helps to eliminate feelings of alienation.

The activities in this program are designed to be self-disclosing. Like caring, self-disclosure is more of a process than a specific kind of activity. The key to encouraging healthy self-disclosure is to begin with activities that are not very threatening and for the facilitator to gently and respectfully support the participants as they self-disclose. Examples of activities for initiating self-disclosure follow.

Sharing No. 1—A personal kaleidoscope. (The following supplies are needed: 5 × 8 cards, pencils, and masking tape.) The facilitator invites the participants to use their pencils to creatively divide a 5 × 8 inch card into three spaces. The participants designate each space as an "A," "B," or "C." In the "A" space, they may draw something that is symbolic of their favorite movie. In the "B" space, they draw something symbolic of their favorite music, and in "C," something symbolic of their favorite meal.

When they have completed their drawings, they attach the card to the upper portion of their body and then are invited to mingle, nonverbally, with the other members of the group. The intent is for all participants to nonverbally share their cards at the same time.

After several minutes of nonverbal sharing, the participants number off (if there are 16 in the group, they number off 1 to 8, so that there are two "1s," two "2s," and so on).

The facilitator invites one person in each dyad (pair) to raise his or her hand. Those who raise their hands have the opportunity to be the first to verbally reveal what their symbols represent. Their partners just listen and give feedback. When they have finished sharing, their partners do the same with their cards.

This is a gentle self-disclosing exercise because the first part is nonverbal and eases the participants into the activity. The verbal part is low in threat because each participant shares with only one other person and not in front of the entire group. Consequently, in the early stages of the curriculum, most of the activities occur in dyads and triads.

The topics are also nonthreatening. If there is one thing people are willing to talk about, it's music. By using nonthreatening topics such as music in a nonthreatening structure, it is possible to reduce fear and increase the likelihood of participation. By discovering it is safe to share low-risk things about ourselves, we become willing to reveal more about who we are, what we want, and what we do or don't understand. Self-disclosure is the first step in the long journey that leads to self-confidence.

Sharing No. 2—Disclosing in pairs. The facilitator invites the group to participate in a process that randomly pairs them with another person. Each pair is seated in a manner conducive to rotating partners in an orderly fashion. A volunteer from each pair is invited to go first in this activity as well as to be the person who will move to a new partner when a new question is asked. A series of timed questions, listed below, are posed. Provision is made for reflection on each question.

The volunteer receives two minutes to speak on the topic in the manner and to the degree desired. The other partner listens. After the 2 minutes have elapsed, the individuals who were to listen demonstrate how well they were listening and comprehending. Then the process is reversed.

After both partners have shared and listened, the person who went first moves to a different partner. (The movement takes place in a clockwise movement, to facilitate orderly exchanges of partners.) After each topic has been covered, the facilitator debriefs the activity by processing awareness, surprises, and discoveries.

Topics:

1. What is your favorite recreational activity? Why?
2. What was your most memorable elementary school experience?
3. If you could change anything about the way you've been taught, what would it be?
4. Describe your favorite vacation.
5. Share an important dream, hope, or goal.
6. Which are the most important books for children to read? Why?

Sharing No. 3—Self-examination. The facilitator pairs up the participants by random method. Then they are invited to reflect upon the following topics:

At this particular time in your life:

A. What are you most *concerned* about?
B. What do you *want* more than anything else?
C. What do you perceive to be your greatest *need*?

After the participants have taken several minutes to reflect on the above, the facilitator asks for a volunteer in each pair. The volunteers will be the listeners and those not volunteering are invited to take the next 4 minutes and share their responses on the above topics. Those sharing do all of the talking while their partners are encouraged to carefully listen.

After 4 minutes have elapsed, the person listening takes 2 minutes and gives feedback. Then the process is reversed.

After the process is completed, the facilitator invites the group to form a circle. The group is then given an opportunity to share what they noticed, found surprising, or discovered.

Sharing No. 4—Statements of conviction. (The following supplies are needed: paper and pencils.) The participants pair up and each records on paper how they would complete the following sentences:

    A. I believe . . .
    B. I should . . .
    C. I need . . .
    D. I want . . .
    E. I have . . .
    F. I will . . .
    G. I am . . .

The partners take turns sharing their statements, alternating on the categories. At the conclusion, the group forms a circle and is given an opportunity to share what they discovered while participating in this activity.

Sharing No. 5—Who are you? (The following supplies are needed: paper and pencils.) The participants are invited to form small groups of three (triads). Each person is designated with an "A," "B," or "C" assignment. "A" asks "B" the question, "Who are you?" "B" answers the question. "C" records "B's" answers on paper.

"A" continues to ask the same question for 3 minutes. After the 3 minutes have elapsed, "C" hands "B" the list of her responses and then each participant shares what she experienced during this phase of the activity.

The participants then switch assignments and the activity continues until each person has performed in all three positions.

Sharing No. 6—Group recall. The facilitator invites the participants to form a circle and to identify, and then reflect upon, their favorite musical group or performer, their favorite color, and their favorite fruit.

After a minute or two for reflection, a volunteer shares his or her preferences and the name this person would like to be known by in the group. The person sitting to the volunteer's left follows, recalling the volunteer's name and then this person's favorite musician, color, and fruit. The exercise continues with each person recalling, in order, the names and favorite choices of the preceding participants before sharing his or her own selections. The exercise is completed with the initiator having to recall what everyone else in the group shared.

Sharing Option 6a—Group recall—"Meeting of great minds." The facilitator invites the participants to form a circle and to consider persons of great historical significance whom they would choose to invite to a special dinner party. Upon choosing someone, they are invited to reflect upon the main course they would serve this individual and the background music they would play.

When everyone is ready, the facilitator explains the process for sharing as follows:

- A volunteer goes first and reveals the person this individual would invite, the main course to be served, and the music to be played.
- The person sitting to the left of the volunteer goes next, first recalling what the volunteer shared and then this person's own choices.
- The activity continues clockwise, each person recalling for the previous participants before sharing personal choices. The activity continues until the person who started the process is reached. The initiator of the process then completes the activity by attempting to recall, for the entire group, what everyone shared.
- In this activity, it is disrespectful to help anyone unless they specifically ask for help.

Additional Group Recall Topics:

A. Activity and music
B. Fruit and state
C. Car and movie
D. Book and hobby

This is an excellent activity for learning everyone's name, in the event the group is not well acquainted. The caring stage is reinforced as the participants demonstrate how effectively they were listening. It is warm and personal, because the person recalling the data looks directly at the individual for whom he or she is recalling and, by using the person's first name, further demonstrates caring. It's little things like using a person's first name that really convey intimacy and caring. In this kind of an atmosphere, people increasingly become willing to self-disclose.

Stage 3: Awareness

Awareness Is the Precondition to Self-Respect

There are many barriers to awareness. Maslow suggests that a primary obstacle is our need for approval from and acceptance by others. When we experience injustice and discrimination, our perception can become faulty and may interfere with a full and clear awareness of reality.

Perception (your capacity to see reality) is the precondition to awareness and is the source from which all behavior emanates. Our self-esteem is grounded in our perception. When we are stigmatized and devalued as human beings, it is difficult to ward off depression and a decline in our performance.

The facilitative approach takes the many barriers to awareness into account by seeking to provide a safe, approving, nonthreatening environment. When the facilitator listens empathically, meaningful contact, which is so essential for becoming aware and promoting positive growth, may be achieved. Authentic presence in the facilitator further expands the climate of trust and promotes discovery in the participants.

At this stage, the emphasis is upon three key elements—*strengths, needs,* and *values*—that are essential for developing an accurate perception. They are fundamental to the acquisition of an integrated self-awareness. Using specific exercises that focus on each of these elements, this program facilitates their individual discovery.

The first of the three to be experienced at this stage is the uncovering of personal strengths. This may be accomplished through getting in touch with past successes. A sense of "I can-ness" is fostered through the reclamation of our positive past. Past success becomes the springboard to future success and may increase our self-confidence.

The following are activities that facilitate recovery of an individual's positive past.

Awareness No. 1—The inquiry process. The facilitator begins by asking the participants: "What kinds of things would you like to know about me that would be meaningful?" As the students respond with questions, the facilitator records them on a chalkboard or newsprint. The facilitator does not edit or discriminate in any way about the questions—treating them all seriously no matter how difficult this becomes. Furthermore, during this stage of recording questions, the facilitator does not answer any of the questions. The intent is to brainstorm questions and allow the process to enable the participants to reflect upon what is a good question. Often, the best answer to a question is an even better question.

The facilitator promotes evaluation of the questions by asking: "If you had answers to the questions listed on the board, which would be most meaningful to you?" When it appears no further questions are forthcoming or sufficient questions have been generated, the facilitator encourages the participants to individually evaluate all of the questions and then choose the question that would provide the most meaningful information.

The participants are then randomly placed in small groups of four persons wherein they reveal the question they individually selected as the best question. Each group is invited to examine, and select by consensus, the question that the group concludes is the best question.

The facilitator then briefly provides an answer to each of the questions posed by the groups. The participants then reassemble in their small groups and process what makes a good question. The activity is concluded with the participants writing a brief essay on how their thinking has changed between when this activity was initiated and when the process was completed. The essays are then shared within the small groups.

The facilitator completes this activity by processing awareness and discoveries with the entire group (Adapted from Victoria Gamber, personal communication, 1973, reprinted with permission).

Awareness No. 2—Public interview questions. (The following supplies are needed: the worksheet [Figure 3.2].) Feelings of alienation and defensiveness frequently block participation in the learning experience. This activity is designed to cultivate a sense of belonging and to reduce defensiveness in the participants.

The facilitator randomly pairs up the participants and invites them to interview one another. A list of questions is provided, but the participants are not restricted to asking the questions on the list. The list is merely to serve as a catalyst for evoking meaningful questions.

A person in each pair volunteers to be interviewed first. The person asking the questions must also be willing to answer any question asked. However, the individual being asked the questions has the option to "pass" on any question and to terminate the interview at any point.

After each participant has been interviewed, the facilitator processes awareness and insights with the participants.

Awareness No. 3—Esteem building. (The following supplies are needed: sheets of 11 × 17-inch paper; drawing supplies, such as crayons, paints, colored pencils, or magic markers; and labels). The participants are invited to reflect and identify seven successes or meaningful accomplishments. These achievements should be occasions in which the participant acted with courage or was particularly creative or productive. The successes may come from any period in the participants' lives. The largeness or smallness of these experiences as perceived by other people is *not* important. What *is* important is that they be meaningful to the participant.

When all participants have identified seven accomplishments and recorded them on a sheet of paper using key words as a guide, each member of the group receives a sheet of 11 × 17-inch paper and access to drawing supplies, such as crayons, paints, colored pencils, magic markers. The participants are then invited to visualize a symbol or geometric shape that

Public Interview Questions

1. How do you tell "right" from "wrong"? "Good" from "bad"?
2. How can you tell if you're doing the right thing?
3. What bothers you most about adults? About young people?
4. What are you most concerned about at this time in your life?
5. Which inventions would we have been better off without?
6. Are you concerned about what's happening to the environment? Why?
7. What do you worry about most?
8. What, if anything, seems to be worth dying for?
9. What is change?
10. What are the primary causes of change?
11. Which are the most important changes taking place in the world now?
12. Who are the most important musicians in the world today?
13. What are the musicians communicating with their music today?
14. What are you interested in at this time in your life?
15. Which are the most important changes necessary with regard to schools?
16. What are the dumbest and most dangerous ideas prevalent today?
17. What are the most important changes occurring during the past 25 years?
18. Who is discriminated against in your community? In which ways?
19. In your perception, which sex has it easier in our culture?
20. What constitutes a "perfect" evening for you?
21. Whom do you most admire? Why?
22. Which ability or quality do you most want to cultivate or acquire? Why?
23. Do you most prefer being around men or women? Why?
24. What are you most grateful for in your life? Why?
25. How would your relationship change if your best friend became HIV positive?
26. Would you like to become famous? Why?
27. Do you want your friends to tell you what they really think of you? Why?
28. Who is the most important person in your life? Why?
29. What do you value most in a relationship? Why?
30. What would you like to be doing 5 years from now? Why?
31. Would you like to be elected president of the United States? Why?
32. For what would you like to be remembered when you die?
33. What are you concerned about more than anything else?
34. What are your greatest needs at this time in your life?
35. What makes you happy? Why?
36. Do you trust the press and what's reported on TV news? Why?
37. What are today's artists trying to tell us?
38. What is your attitude toward high school, college, and professional sports?
39. Should the United States undertake a human landing on Mars? Why?
40. Should we encourage people to "buy" American? Why?

Figure 3.2.

SOURCE: From Teaching as a Subversive Activity by Neil Postman and Charles Weingartner. Copyright © 1969 by Neil Postman and Charles Weingartner. Used by permission of Dell Books, a division of Bantam Doubleday Dell Publishing Group, Inc.

captures the essence of their seven accomplishments and to draw this symbol on their paper.

When the drawing is completed, the participants receive a supply of labels and the facilitator invites the group to form a circle for sharing their accomplishments with one another. Someone volunteers to go first while the remaining group members listen and write down on the labels impressions or perceptions they have of the volunteer's positive strengths. Because what they are recording on the labels are perceptions, the participants are free to write whatever emerges in their awareness. They are to avoid using qualifying words and negative characteristics.

When the volunteer has completed sharing past successes, the paper with the symbol drawn on it is sent around the group. The group members take turns vocally expressing what they have written as they apply their labels on the back side of the volunteer's drawing.

When all of the labels have been applied, the volunteer receives an opportunity to share whatever this individual became aware of from this activity.

Another person volunteers and the activity continues in this manner until everyone has had an opportunity to participate.

This is a strength bombardment activity. It is a powerful experience for the person giving the "positive feedback" (impressions of strengths perceived) as well as for the person who is receiving it. This activity always proves to be very meaningful for the participants (Adapted from *Achievement Motivation Program*, 1971).

Awareness No. 4—Reviewing the previous 24 hours. The facilitator invites the participants to do the following:

Close your eyes and concentrate on relaxing your body. Let go of any feelings you have and release every thought that comes to you. Your mind should be quiet and receptive while remaining alert. Now, reflect back over the previous 24 hours and, in your mind, play them back like a movie running in reverse, beginning with the present moment. Throughout this experience it is important to maintain, as much as possible, the attitude of an objective observer. Become neither elated at success nor depressed and unhappy about failure. The aim is not to relive the experience but to noncritically register in your consciousness the patterns and meaning of the last 24 hours (Adapted from Kull, 1977).

After 5 minutes have elapsed, the facilitator invites the participants to open their eyes and to write down impressions of positive moments they uncovered during their review of the past 24 hours. These would be moments when they discovered they were engaged in a particularly meaningful activity or when they made a positive difference with their actions.

The facilitator then invites the group to form a circle and to share newfound awareness.

Through assisting the participants to become more aware of their strengths, they gain new insight into their potential. This activity encourages participants and increases their self-respect and their respect for others. Gaining awareness of personal strengths causes you to be more courageous, more willing to risk self-disclosure. And this experience empowers you to confront your needs.

The following three activities assist with the identification of needs.

Awareness No. 5—Identification of needs. (The following supplies are needed: pencils and worksheet [Figure 3.3].) This activity is designed to help the participants pinpoint their individual needs. The facilitator begins by providing the participants with the brief introduction to Maslow's "Hierarchy of Needs," which follows.

Abraham Maslow, in his study of highly successful people, found these self-actualizing individuals had satisfied their basic needs and were motivated in transcendent ways because they were free from struggling to fulfill the lower needs. Maslow listed the basic needs in a hierarchical manner. He organized them in terms of the degree to which satisfaction of each is a prerequisite to the search for satisfaction of the next need. Maslow categorized these needs into two classes: survival needs and growth needs. The survival needs are (a) *physiological,* the most powerful and basic of all our needs, that is, the need for food, liquid, and anything that is essential to the preservation of life; (b) *safety,* security from the elements and threat from other human beings; (c) *belongingness and love,* to experience being loved by, and loving, the significant individuals in a person's life; and (d) *self-esteem,* the desire for achievement, confidence, competence, and self-appreciation.

The *growth* needs, or "being motives" as Maslow called them, are (e) *knowledge and understanding,* the desire to comprehend, to systematize, to organize, to analyze, and to see relationships; (f) *aesthetic appreciation,* the love of beauty and harmony; and (g) *self-actualization,* the desire to create, to realize more potential, and to live life with purpose and meaning.

The facilitator provides the appropriate worksheet (Figure 3.3) with Maslow's "Hierarchy of Needs" listed on the left and a related philosophical question opposite each need on the right. The participants are encouraged to examine their own most basic needs and to record answers to the questions appearing on the worksheet.

The facilitator, through a chance procedure, pairs the participants and provides a 5-minute time period in which each participant may share and give feedback. After sufficient time to reflect upon this portion of the activity, the group is invited to reassemble in a circle and to share what they have uncovered.

Through asking questions like these—"What did you notice?" "What did you discover as you looked over these questions?" "Are there any

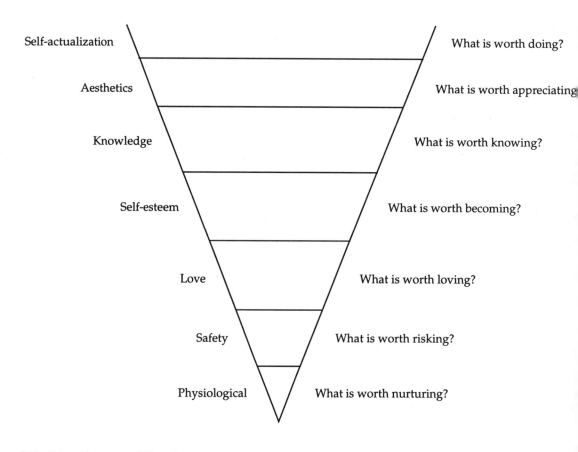

Figure 3.3. Identification of Needs

surprises?"—the facilitator assists the participants with uncovering their most basic needs.

The worksheet is symbolic. The base of the triangle is enclosed, indicating that there is a finite quantity of our essential physiological needs. The specific needs—that is, oxygen, water, food, sleep, and so on—are relatively few in number when compared with the other levels of need. As they proceed up the ladder of needs, the participants discover an increasing number of needs from which to choose. The top of this inverted triangle is open, indicating our unlimited potential for growth and intentional living.

Need-identification activities are instrumental in facilitating self-discovery for meaningful living. This activity particularly helps the participants to understand the hierarchical nature of our needs.

Awareness No. 6—Shoulds/Oughts. The facilitator invites the participants to make a list of the "shoulds" or "oughts" about which their conscience is nagging them.

Next, the facilitator brainstorms with the participants all of the "slippery" ways in which they have been avoiding accomplishing these tasks or "shoulds." Typical slippery expressions include *maybe, possibly, I can't, perhaps, tomorrow, when I feel like it, yes—but, if only, I'm thinking about it, I don't have time, I don't have enough money,* and so on.

The participants are randomly paired with another person and share with their partner one of their shoulds/oughts. They work together through the following structure: Partner "A" provides Partner "B" with one of the shoulds from "A's" list of seven "I shoulds" (e.g., *"I should stop smoking").* Partner "B" takes that statement and changes it to *"You should stop smoking."* "A" responds as she naturally would; (e.g., *"I'm trying to . . ."* or *"I've been thinking about it").* The main thing is for "A" to experience being as slippery as she can be.

"B" continues to repeat over and over the "should" statement—"You should stop smoking"—until "A" responds in one of three possible ways:

1. "No—I will not."
2. "Yes—I will."
3. "I'm not ready to deal with that yet."

If the response is either #1 or #3, the activity does not continue. However, if "A" responds with "Yes—I will," "B" continues by attempting to secure specific information, for example, when, where, and how "A" will stop smoking. When this has been identified in a direct and nonslippery manner, "B" proceeds by uncovering if "A" is willing to make a commitment with another person in the room to "stop smoking." This concludes the first half of this activity. The process is then reversed for the partners.

The activity concludes with the facilitator processing awareness. (Adapted from Frederic M. Hudson, personal communication, 1977. Reprinted with permission.)

Awareness No. 7—A symphony of needs. The facilitator invites the participants to form a circle and to make a list of seven needs of which they are aware at this time in their lives, for example, *"I need to be more patient." "I need to be more of a risk taker." "I need more money." "I need love." "I need a new car." "I need to read more." "I need a vacation."*

After the participants have completed their lists, the facilitator invites them to form a circle. A volunteer moves into the center of the circle and shares her list of needs with the group, then selects seven persons and assigns a different need to each person.

An eighth person is selected by the volunteer to function as a "conductor of the symphony" while the volunteer sits in the middle of the circle with eyes closed. The seven individuals selected by the volunteer function as musicians in this symphony and perform their parts at the discretion of the "conductor." They vocalize the need assigned to them by the person sitting in the middle of the circle when the "conductor" brings them into the performance. In conjunction with the conductor, they choose the voice and modulation they perceive as appropriate for their part.

The symphony of needs is conducted for 2 or 3 minutes. This is followed by a period of silence during which the volunteer continues to remain in the circle with eyes closed, checking out new awareness and insights.

The activity continues until all have received an opportunity to participate. The facilitator then processes awareness. Need-identification activities facilitate the discovery of what is essential and what is not essential for quality living. They contribute to a deeper understanding of the hierarchical nature of our needs.

The third level of awareness is an examination of the fundamental values that from antiquity have been the core of every culture and major religion. Through assisting the participants to become more familiar with universal values and to reflect upon personal values, this program enables the participants to become more familiar with ethics and the characteristics of good persons.

The following are six activities that cultivate a deeper awareness of the fundamental values. (Adapted from Frederic M. Hudson, personal communication, 1977. Reprinted with permission.)

Awareness No. 8—The filter by which we color our lives. The participants are invited to pair up with another person. A series of timed questions that follow are posed to the pairs and they receive a couple of minutes for reflection.

A volunteer in each pair is invited to share for 3 minutes on the first topic, to the degree and manner desired. The volunteer's partner only listens. After 3 minutes, the listeners demonstrate how well they understood what they heard by giving feedback to their partner. Then, the process is reversed.

All pairs are seated in a manner conducive to changing partners in an orderly manner. After each person has shared and listened, the volunteer moves to a different partner. After all topics have been examined, the facilitator processes the activity by examining awareness, surprises, and insights.

Topics:

1. How have you become the kind of person you are?
2. In which ways and to what degree have you become the person you had hoped to become?
3. What are values? What do they have to do with morality, ethics, and character development?

4. To what degree do you believe you possess free choice? Were your values inherited or programmed into your genes?

5. How have you arrived at your personal set of beliefs? Which are your primary values?

Awareness No. 9—Assessing influences shaping values. (The following supplies are needed: pencils and worksheets [Figure 3.4a and Figure 3.4b].) This activity enables the participants to uncover the source of their fundamental values. The participants complete the "Assessment of Influences Shaping Your Values" instrument and then search for meaning and understanding in the choices they made through studying the information provided based upon the research of Hunter Lewis (1990).

The facilitator uses a random process for pairing the participants. They share insights and issues raised through participation in this activity. The activity is completed by processing awareness with the entire group.

Awareness No. 10—Being Values Card Sort. (The following supplies are needed: scissors, the "Being Values Card Sort" [Figure 3.5], paper, and pencils.) The participants are invited to separate the values cards found on the worksheet and to classify them according to the three categories of (a) very important, (b) important, and (c) not as important. Next, the participants rank order the cards in each category by arranging the cards in the stack from most to least important. After ranking the values, the participants list all 21 values on a sheet of paper for future reference in the activities that follow. The facilitator processes awareness after all of the participants have completed this activity (Adapted from the *Achievement Motivation Program*, 1971).

Awareness No. 11—Five-Sort Values Inventory. The facilitator provides each participant with the "Five-Sort Values Inventory" worksheet (Figure 3.6) and a pencil. Each grouping contains five values. In the parentheses preceding each value, place a number from 1 to 5. Number 1 represents your highest ranking value in that group; number 5 represents the value you rank lowest. Number all values; a different rating must be given each value listed in a group of five.

To summarize the results, enter the numbers recorded on the "Five-Sort Values Inventory" (Figure 3.6) on the "Values Inventory Rating Summary" worksheet (Figure 3.7). Each value appears five times. The participants will have recorded 21 sets of five entries for each value.

By adding the numbers recorded for each value, you will produce a weighted score for each value. The lower the number total, the higher that value ranks in priority.

The 21 values are force-ranked against each other five times. Definitions of the values are found on page 57 (Adapted from the *Achievement Motivation Program*, 1971).

Assessment of Influences Shaping Your Values

Within each group below, rank order (1, 2, 3, 4, 5, & 6) the influence each item would have, in comparison to the other items, in shaping your values system for everyday life. Use a (1) for most influence and a (6) for least influence.

_____ 1. A minister, priest, or rabbi

_____ 2. A college professor of logic

_____ 3. An artist

_____ 4. A consumer advocate

_____ 5. An astrologer

_____ 6. A medical doctor

_____ 1. The Bible or Koran

_____ 2. An investigative writer

_____ 3. A poet

_____ 4. A social reformer

_____ 5. A New Age psychologist

_____ 6. A physicist

_____ 1. A police officer

_____ 2. A philosopher

_____ 3. A musician

_____ 4. A family member

_____ 5. A practitioner of meditation

_____ 6. A social scientist

_____ 1. An acclaimed teacher

_____ 2. A skilled debater

_____ 3. A best-selling author

_____ 4. A motivational speaker

_____ 5. A psychic

_____ 6. A chemist

_____ 1. The President of the United States

_____ 2. A mathematician

_____ 3. An essayist

_____ 4. An environmentalist

_____ 5. A tarot card reader

_____ 6. A psychiatrist

_____ 1. A superintendent of schools

_____ 2. An investigative reporter

_____ 3. An architect

_____ 4. A counselor

_____ 5. A practitioner of yoga

_____ 6. A biologist

To score your profile, add up the rankings you awarded each of the (1s) and record the total below in the appropriate category. Continue in like manner with each of the remaining numbers. The _lowest total_ reveals the category having the greatest influence on your values system and the _highest total_ is indicative of the least influential category.

Category #1: **Authority**

    Total Score: _____   Rank: _____

Category #2: **Logic**

    Total Score: _____   Rank: _____

Category #3: **Sense Experience**

    Total Score: _____   Rank: _____

Category #4: **Emotion**

    Total Score: _____   Rank: _____

Category #5: **Intuition**

    Total Score: _____   Rank: _____

Category #6: **Science**

    Total Score: _____   Rank: _____

Figure 3.4a.

SOURCE: Andersen. _Courageous Teaching._ © 1995 Corwin Press, Inc. Reprinted with permission.

Six Ways We Choose Values

Mode by Which We Arrive at Knowledge	Explanation	Summary
1. Authority	Taking someone else's word, having faith in an external authority. For example, having faith in a church or the bible.	I place my faith in a church authority (i.e., Pope).
2. Logic	Reasoning things out in your own mind. Subjecting your beliefs to a variety of consistency tests that underlie deductive reasoning.	Because A is true, B must be true because B follows from A.
3. Sense experience	Gaining direct knowledge through your own senses. Seeing for yourself and then processing your experience.	I know it's true because I saw it, I heard it, I tasted it, and so on.
4. Emotion	Feeling that something is right: We may not always associate feeling with thinking or judging, but in reality we *think* and *judge* through our emotions much of the time.	I just "feel" that this is true.
5. Intuition	The act or faculty of knowing without the use of rational processes. The human capacity to apprehend in totality a given situation. Located in the unconscious mind, intuition is a means for seeing within or receiving a vision.	After struggling with this problem all day, I went to bed confused and exhausted. The next morning, as I awakened, the solution came to me in a flash.
6. Science	A precise technique that relies on sense experience to collect the observable facts, intuition to develop a testable hypothesis about the facts, logic to develop the test (experiment), and sense experience again to complete the test.	I tested the hypothesis experimentally and found it was true.

Figure 3.4b.
SOURCE: Adapted Figure 3.5: "SIX WAYS WE CHOOSE VALUES" from A QUESTION OF VALUES by HUNTER LEWIS. Copyright © 1990 by Hunter Lewis. Reprinted by permission of HarperCollins Publishers, Inc.

Being Values Card Sort

Aliveness: The state or quality of being fully alive. Abundant energy.	**Love:** Unselfish devotion, deep affection and enthusiasm in relationships.	**Simplicity:** Free from unnecessary desires and attachments without guile. Unpretentious.
Altruism: Profound regard for other people. Willing to act on the behalf of people needing help.	**Necessity:** Acceptance of the inevitable that is, death, obligations, natural disasters, and so on.	**Spiritual Growth:** Care of the soul and concern for the sacred. Seeking higher consciousness.
Beauty: Appreciation for experiences that provide a simultaneous sense of joy and peace.	**Order:** Purposeful, meaningful, intentional, natural, balanced, harmonious, and so on.	**Truth:** Genuineness, honesty, transparency, sincerity in character, openness, and so on.
Dichotomy-Transcendence: Able to see the whole picture by rising above polar opposites; either/or, this/that, right/wrong.	**Perfection:** The state of being complete, at peace, full of grace, beauty, high quality, and so on.	**Uniqueness:** Original, legitimate, creative, new, surprising, unusual, out of the ordinary, and so on.
Effortlessness: Going with the natural flow of events; free from stress, tension, or hyperactivity.	**Playfulness:** Natural, spontaneous, relaxed, sense of humor, creative, at ease, and so on.	**Wholeness:** Complete, embracing everything, fulfilled, rising above pettiness, being small, and so on.
Ethics: The desire to do the right thing because it is right. Integrity, morality, and character.	**Richness:** Abundance or superior qualities, complete, mature, fulfilled, and so on.	**Willpower:** Inner strength, purposeful, determination, free from social pressure and vanity.
Justice: The condition of equality, fairness; without favoritism or partiality.	**Self-Sufficiency:** Able to respond effectively in any situation; mature, competent, skillful, and so on.	**Wisdom:** Discernment, common sense, keen insight, good judgment, wise, and so on.

Figure 3.5.
SOURCE: Adapted from the *Achievement Motivation Program*, 1971.

Five-Sort Values Inventory

1 ( ) Self-Sufficiency
( ) Altruism
( ) Justice
( ) Spiritual Growth
( ) Wholeness

8 ( ) Necessity
( ) Simplicity
( ) Richness
( ) Wholeness
( ) Wisdom

15 ( ) Beauty
( ) Altruism
( ) Uniqueness
( ) Simplicity
( ) Perfection

2 ( ) Altruism
( ) Necessity
( ) Order
( ) Willpower
( ) Dichotomy-
      Transcendence

9 ( ) Truth
( ) Effortlessness
( ) Willpower
( ) Perfection
( ) Wholeness

16 ( ) Simplicity
( ) Justice
( ) Effortlessness
( ) Aliveness
( ) Dichotomy-
      Transcendence

3 ( ) Uniqueness
( ) Love
( ) Playfulness
( ) Wholeness
( ) Dichotomy-
      Transcendence

10 ( ) Self-Sufficiency
( ) Simplicity
( ) Love
( ) Ethics
( ) Willpower

17 ( ) Altruism
( ) Richness
( ) Effortlessness
( ) Ethics
( ) Playfulness

4 ( ) Beauty
( ) Justice
( ) Playfulness
( ) Willpower
( ) Wisdom

11 ( ) Beauty
( ) Necessity
( ) Effortlessness
( ) Love
( ) Spiritual Growth

18 ( ) Ethics
( ) Wisdom
( ) Spiritual Growth
( ) Perfection
( ) Dichotomy-
      Transcendence

5 ( ) Altruism
( ) Truth
( ) Love
( ) Aliveness
( ) Wisdom

12 ( ) Beauty
( ) Order
( ) Ethics
( ) Aliveness
( ) Wholeness

19 ( ) Simplicity
( ) Truth
( ) Order
( ) Playfulness
( ) Spiritual Growth

6 ( ) Self-Sufficiency
( ) Beauty
( ) Richness
( ) Truth
( ) Dichotomy-
      Transcendence

13 ( ) Uniqueness
( ) Richness
( ) Aliveness
( ) Willpower
( ) Spiritual Growth

20 ( ) Self-Sufficiency
( ) Uniqueness
( ) Effortlessness
( ) Order
( ) Wisdom

7 ( ) Self-Sufficiency
( ) Necessity
( ) Aliveness
( ) Playfulness
( ) Perfection

14 ( ) Richness
( ) Justice
( ) Love
( ) Order
( ) Perfection

21 ( ) Necessity
( ) Uniqueness
( ) Truth
( ) Justice
( ) Ethics

Figure 3.6.
SOURCE: Adapted from the *Achievement Motivation Program*, 1971.

Values Inventory Rating Summary

						Totals
1. Aliveness						
2. Altruism						
3. Beauty						
4. Dichotomy-Transcendence						
5. Effortlessness						
6. Ethics						
7. Justice						
8. Love						
9. Necessity						
10. Order						
11. Perfection						
12. Playfulness						
13. Richness						
14. Self-Sufficiency						
15. Simplicity						
16. Spiritual Growth						
17. Truth						
18. Uniqueness						
19. Wholeness						
20. Willpower						
21. Wisdom						

Figure 3.7.
SOURCE: Adapted from the *Achievement Motivation Program*, 1971.

Definitions of Values:

Aliveness: The state or quality of being fully alive. An abundance of energy.

Altruism: Devotion to and profound regard for other people.

Beauty: An experience that gives a sense of joy and a sense of peace simultaneously. A timeless sense of wonder and awe.

Dichotomy-transcendence: The capacity to rise above polar opposites, either/or, this/that situations.

Effortlessness: Calm, easy, without force.

Ethics: Concern for doing the "right thing" because it is right. Moral.

Justice: Without partiality or favoritism—the condition of fairness.

Love: Unselfish devotion and unconditional acceptance.

Necessity: Acceptance of the inevitable; that is, death, obligations, nature, and so on.

Order: Purposeful, meaningful, intentional, natural, and so on.

Perfection: The state of being complete. Quality.

Playfulness: Natural, spontaneous, relaxed, sense of humor, and so on.

Richness: Abundance of superior qualities.

Self-sufficiency: The ability to effectively respond in any situation. Mature.

Simplicity: Unpretentious. Straightforward, without guile, freedom from unnecessary desires and attachments.

Spiritual growth: Care of the soul and concern for the sacred. Seeking a higher state of consciousness.

Truth: Genuineness, honesty, accuracy, sincerity in character.

Uniqueness: Original, creative, unusual, on the "cutting edge," and so on.

Wholeness: Complete, embracing the "All," fulfilled, above pettiness, and so on.

Willpower: Inner strength, character, purposeful, free from social pressure and vanity, and so on.

Wisdom: Discernment, common sense, good judgment, keen insight, and so on.

Awareness No. 12—Being values auction. (The following supplies are needed: worksheet [Figure 3.8] and pencils.) The participants receive a copy of the "Being Values Auction" worksheet and are informed they have $100,000 to use toward the purchase of the items listed. The facilitator suggests the participants scan the 34 items to determine which items they are most interested in purchasing.

Next, the participants allocate, proportionate to the perceived value of the item, the portion of their $100,000 that they are prepared to spend. In this way a budget is prepared. To expedite this process, all budgeting must be in round figures of $1,000.

Upon completing the budgeting, the facilitator begins to auction off the items. The participants are free to bid on any item, regardless of budgeting for it. During the auction, each individual keeps a record of the items

Being Values Auction

Items for Sale	Amount Budgeted	Maximum Bid	Items Purchased
1. To be free from illness and to have unlimited energy			
2. To volunteer for a year of service to Habitat for Humanity			
3. To live overlooking the ocean on the world's most beautiful beach			
4. To free the world from all prejudice and bigotry			
5. To live without stress, pressures, tension, and demands			
6. To live in a community where everyone lives by the Golden Rule			
7. To have a life-long, fulfilling romantic relationship			
8. To learn to accept that everything is unfolding as it should			
9. To have meaningful work helping to make this a better world			
10. A year off in which to sail around the world with a special friend			
11. To be recognized as the leading authority in my profession			
12. To learn to live with less, free from unnecessary wants and desires			
13. To spend a year in spiritual study with all personal needs met			
14. To resolve all my problems and to make only good decisions			
15. To acquire the courage to speak out when it counts			
16. To have more quality time with my friends and family			
17. To discover a cure for AIDS			
18. To obtain social equality for all people			
19. To work where no one gossips and everyone is open and honest			
20. To live in a world where everyone respects the environment			
21. To win the Boston Marathon			
22. To help rid the world of poverty			
23. To live in a house designed by the world's leading architect			
24. To find a way to end all racism in America			
25. To be a positive role model for all young people			
26. To give and receive unconditional love			
27. To live an exciting life and die free from all worries			
28. To find the meaning of life			
29. To perform with one of the leading musical groups in the world			
30. To be recognized for my competency and skill			
31. To live off the land on a remote island			
32. To spend a year with the spiritual teacher of my choice			
33. To realize my full potential and be true to myself			
34. To write a best-selling book			

Figure 3.8.
SOURCE: Adapted from the *Achievement Motivation Program*, 1971.

on which he or she is bidding, recording the highest amount bid for each item.

The facilitator auctions off the items in the traditional manner. The items are selected at random for auction rather than in the sequence they are listed.

After the items have been auctioned, the facilitator invites the participants to examine each item and to determine the intrinsic values that appear to them to be in the items they were interested in purchasing. The author perceives the items are related to values as follows (*Achievement Motivation Program*, 1971):

ITEM	VALUE
1 & 21	Aliveness
2 & 22	Altruism
3 & 23	Beauty
4 & 24	Dichotomy-transcendence
5	Effortlessness
6 & 25	Ethics
7 & 26	Love
8 & 27	Necessity
9 & 28	Order
10 & 29	Playfulness
11 & 30	Self-sufficiency
12 & 31	Simplicity
13 & 32	Spiritual growth
14	Wisdom
15	Willpower
16	Richness
33	Wholeness
17 & 34	Uniqueness

Awareness No. 13—Life Markers. The facilitator distributes the "Life Markers" worksheet (Figure 3.9) and pencils to the participants and invites them to complete this instrument.

For each of the 10 categories, the participants identify the most important belief they hold and, using a few key words, record this belief in the appropriate box. Next, the participants identify the person(s) or group most influential or responsible for the position they currently hold on each value area identified. Third, the participants indicate the degree to which they prize each value. And, fourth, the participants rank order the 10 value areas.

After completing the worksheet, the participants are invited to form small groups of four persons by numbering off 1 to 4. Number "1" begins by sharing a position on any or all of the value areas. Number "2" listens and will later have an opportunity to demonstrate how effectively she

Life Markers

The most important belief I hold about each of the values listed below:	The person or group I learned it from:	The degree to which I prize what I believe:					Rank
ETHICS		1	2	3	4	5	
BEAUTY		1	2	3	4	5	
LOVE		1	2	3	4	5	
CREATIVITY		1	2	3	4	5	
HONESTY		1	2	3	4	5	
JUSTICE		1	2	3	4	5	
PURPOSEFULNESS		1	2	3	4	5	
RESPECT		1	2	3	4	5	
RESPONSIBILITY		1	2	3	4	5	
WISDOM		1	2	3	4	5	

Figure 3.9.

Source: Andersen. *Courageous Teaching*. © 1995 Corwin Press, Inc. Reprinted with permission.

understood what Number "1" was expressing. Number "3" is an observer and serves as a backup to Number "2." Number "4" pays attention to her feelings and will later reveal what she became aware of or noticed while listening to Number "1."

The participants receive an opportunity to engage in each of the described roles. Three minutes are provided for the participants to function in role "1" and two minutes for each of the other roles.

The activity is concluded with the participants forming a circle and the facilitator processing awareness.

The facilitative approach helps participants uncover what they have already learned about important values and assists them with deepening their appreciation for the concepts of love, honesty, ethics, justice, beauty, responsibility, and so on. It is an opportunity to examine the values that are universally prized by all cultures and religions and to experience their social impact.

An awareness of personal strengths, needs, and universal values provides a basis for the growth and development of healthy self-respect and respect for others. When you begin to understand what is unique, special, and good about yourself and others, self-esteem and respect increase.

Stage 4: Respect

Respect Is the Precondition to Faith

Self-respect is generated by discovering what is good about yourself and through experiencing your potential for doing that which is "good." Examples of activities that cultivate healthy respect follow.

Respect No. 1—A time capsule. Prior to the time when this activity takes place, the facilitator invites the participants to reflect upon their lives and to think about certain articles in their possession that have special meaning. These articles should be reflective of meaningful experiences, accomplishments, stepping stones, friendships, memories, artistic creations, anything indicative of who and what they are really like as persons. The articles selected for placement in this time capsule would, in a distant time, give the finder a true picture of what is precious to or about the participant. In instances where it is not practical to bring the real article, the participants may bring a picture, photo, or draw something that is symbolic.

On the day of the activity, the facilitator invites the participants to bring their time capsules with them and to form a circle. The participants are offered an opportunity to share the five articles they have placed in their time capsule with the group.

As the participants reach into their time capsules, they are in essence revealing precious information about themselves. The participants may pass their articles around the group for closer inspection.

The activity is concluded with the facilitator processing awareness, insights, and discoveries.

Respect No. 2—Precious memories. In this activity, the participants have an opportunity to reexperience periods in their lives that were occasions for increasing their sense of self-respect. The facilitator invites the participants to sit in a circle and reflect upon those times when they were especially pleased with their performance or behavior, events when they "rose to the occasion" and were at their very best for the situation.

It may have been a time when the participants were especially sensitive, compassionate, brave, honest, or just did the "right thing."

This activity affords the participants an opportunity to get in touch with their positive past. It is an opportunity for them to appreciate what they are really capable of being, doing, and knowing.

Participation in this activity affords the participants an opportunity to increase their respect for one another. The facilitator begins by inviting a volunteer to begin sharing. Should no one volunteer, the facilitator reads from a list of prepared topics that may evoke responses from the participants concerning times when they were particularly pleased with their behavior. Some possible topics follow:

- A time when you surprised someone with the perfect gift.
- A time when you were honest in a difficult situation.
- A time when you did something about discrimination or prejudice.
- A time when you helped a friend in need.
- A time when you realized a dream or goal.
- A time when you did something that benefited the environment.
- A time when you didn't give up but "stayed the course."
- A time when you exercised self-discipline.
- A time when you assisted a disadvantaged person.
- A time when you had the courage to stand alone.

When all of the participants have received an opportunity to share, the facilitator processes awareness, surprises, and discoveries.

Respect No. 3—Resentments/appreciations exercise. (The following supplies are needed: paper and pencils.) Because contact with others may prove to be painful, we begin to curb our spontaneous behavior and wrap layers of defense about our person. This process typically begins at a very early age. As very small children, we come to recognize that the significant others (family, school, church, and so on) in our life have great expectations as to how we ought to be, do, and think. We discover that we get rewarded when we please others and punished when we go against their wishes. This causes us to give up much of our natural behavior and to replace natural behavior with what we sense will be acceptable behavior. Consequently, we begin to lose touch with what we really want and who we really are. We repress our emotions, physical behavior, and thoughts because we have learned it is frequently painful to let others discover us as we really are. Repression of feelings, thoughts, and movement affects our balance and shows up in our body structure and personality development. And, through distancing ourselves from others, we, too, become self-alienated.

The participants receive a sheet of paper and are invited to identify an issue, problem, or concern on which they have strong feelings of resentment. They begin by listing all of the resentments relating to the issue. Next the participants address the (issue, problem, or concern) by listing what they appreciate.

When they can't think of any more appreciations, they return to their resentment list and see what else (new) they resent about the (issue, problem, or concern). Then they look over the appreciation list and see if any new appreciations can be added.

The participants are encouraged to look over their list of resentments and rank order them. Next, they rank order their appreciations.

Then the participants look at the two ranked lists and place each item on a continuum, with either the most important resentment or the most important appreciation listed first, and the second most important resentment/appreciation listed second, and so on until all are ranked on a continuum.

The facilitator then invites the participants to form a circle and share new insights, discoveries, and surprises (Perls, 1969).

Respect No. 4—Here/there exercise. The facilitator invites the participants to sit in a circle, close their eyes, and go away in their imagination to the person they would like to be. After 2 minutes, the participants are invited to return to the "here," the here and now, and compare the two situations, choosing which is preferable.

With their eyes still closed, the participants are invited to go away in their imaginations again to the person they would most like to be and identify the primary characteristics of this person. What are the qualities, personality traits, that are most admired in the ideal person?

After 2 minutes, the participants are invited to return again to the "here and now" and note any surprises, discoveries, and insights. Next, the facilitator invites the participants to go away and return again and again in this fantasy until they feel comfortable in the present situation and aware of what is missing in their lives, what they want to change, what they need, and so on.

When they know the answers to these questions, they are invited to write a brief essay describing what they discovered. Then, the facilitator invites the participants to form a circle and share whatever they may choose with the entire group. The activity is completed with the facilitator processing awareness with the entire group.

Respect No. 5—Early recollections. (The following supplies are needed: paper and pencils.) Each participant receives a sheet of paper and is invited to list as many ethnic/cultural recollections he or she can recall from early childhood.

The participants are next encouraged to reflect upon their lists and uncover the degree to which each of the recollections remains a precious memory and a part of their cultural heritage that they still practice.

The participants are then invited to form a circle and share with the group discoveries and surprises they have received from this activity.

Respect No. 6—Assumptions and expectations. (The following supplies are needed: paper and pencils.) The participants are invited to number off and form groups of three. Within each group of three, a person is designated an "A," another as "B," and the third person as "C."

"A" begins by asking "B" one of the questions listed below. "C" listens and records the responses "B" makes. "A" *actively listens* to "B" and demonstrates the degree to which "A" understood what "B" said after the question has been asked repeatedly 10 times. "C" completes the first round of this activity by sharing anything that "A" missed and then gives "B" a copy of the written responses.

Each participant receives an opportunity to function in all of the roles. After each has participated as "A," "B," and "C," the activity is concluded with all of the participants forming a circle and sharing with the group what they noticed, discovered, or were surprised by through participating in this activity.

Questions:

1. Describe an Asian.
2. Describe a black.
3. Describe a Latino.
4. Describe a Native American.
5. Describe a white.
6. Describe a male.
7. Describe a female.
8. Describe a handicapped person.
9. Describe an elderly person.
10. Describe a homeless person.

Respect No. 7—Monstrous acts of inhumanity. (The following supplies are needed: worksheet [Figure 3.10] and pencils.) The facilitator invites the participants to reflect upon instances in history that demonstrate inhumanity by human beings, listing two examples for each of the categories identified on the "Monstrous Acts of Inhumanity" worksheet. The participants are to indicate their perceptions of what *motivated* the injustices as well as what the *payoff* was for the perpetrator.

Upon completing the worksheet, the participants are invited to form groups of four persons and to identify themselves as an "A," "B," "C," or "D." "A" begins by sharing with the three other participants. When "A" finishes or after 2 minutes have elapsed, "B" demonstrates how well he or she was listening by giving "A" feedback. Then "B" shares his or her list with the group during the next 2 minutes while "C" listens and gives feedback, and so on.

After each has shared and given feedback, the facilitator invites the group to form a circle and to share anything noticed or found to be surprising.

Respect No. 8—A comparison of similarities and differences. The participants are invited to number off and form groups of three. The facilitator invites one person in each small group to volunteer. The volunteer initiates the process by sharing on one of the topic(s) that follow. As soon as the volunteer has completed sharing, the person sitting to the left of the volunteer provides feedback. The activity continues in like manner until each person has provided feedback prior to sharing a personal position on one of the topics.

Sharing should be limited to 2 minutes and feedback to 1 minute. The participants form new small groups of three persons for each of the following topics:

Monstrous Acts of Inhumanity

Category	Act of Inhumanity	Motivation	Payoff
International	1. 2.		
National	1. 2.		
State	1. 2.		
Local	1. 2.		
Personal	1. 2.		

Figure 3.10.
SOURCE: Andersen. *Courageous Teaching*. © 1995 Corwin Press, Inc. Reprinted with permission.

1. What do *sports* have to say about the similarities/differences between African, Asian, Latino, and Native American cultures?

2. What does *music* have to say about the similarities/differences between African, Asian, Latino, and Native American cultures?

3. What do the *visual arts* have to say about the similarities/differences between African, Asian, Latino, and Native American cultures?

4. What do *poetry and literature* have to say about the similarities/differences between African, Asian, Latino, and Native American cultures?

5. What do *science and technology* have to say about the similarities/differences between African, Asian, Latino, and Native American cultures?

6. What does *religion* have to say about the similarities/differences between African, Asian, Latino, and Native American cultures?

7. What does *family* have to say about the similarities/differences between African, Asian, Latino, and Native American cultures?

8. What does *education* have to say about the similarities/differences between African, Asian, Latino, and Native American cultures?

9. What do *industry and the labor force* have to say about the similarities/differences between African, Asian, Latino, and Native American cultures?

After each person has shared and demonstrated an understanding, the facilitator invites the participants to form a circle and to share discoveries and meaningful awareness.

Respect No. 9—Do schools have a moral obligation? The facilitator provides an opportunity for the participants to pair up and then invites them to consider the following: "Regardless of any legal requirements, do you perceive schools have a moral or ethical obligation to integrate equity principles into the classroom?" The participants receive 3 minutes to share their position and one minute to provide feedback on what their partner shared. Then the activity is concluded by re-forming a circle and affording the participants an opportunity to share what they uncovered.

Upon completing this activity, the facilitator may share pro/con positions on the case for moral education in our schools. This is an appropriate time to examine such issues as the Holocaust, the internment of Japanese Americans in concentration camps during World War II, segregation, and so on.

Self-respect is generated by the discovery of what is good about ourselves and other people and by experiencing our potential for doing that which is "good." Self-respect serves as a precondition to faith. Without self-respect, there is little hope for the future. Faith arises and grows out of our positive personal experiences, which are the source of self-respect. Self-respect increases our inner strength. The intent of these activities is to empower teachers with the means for giving students new reasons for being optimistic about their future.

Stage 5: Faith

Faith Is the Precondition to Responsibility

This approach is not concerned with dogma or religious beliefs but, instead, with facilitating the growth of a sustaining sense of optimism, hope, or faith. In this program, "how" the facilitator is with the participants is much more important than "what" the facilitator does, that is, the activities used. Few things are more encouraging than being with someone who has faith in you.

Nevertheless, there are certain group process activities that can contribute to students becoming more optimistic about their future. The following activities are designed to increase the development of faith.

Faith No. 1—The microlab. The facilitator invites the participants to form two separate groups, equal in number. This may be accomplished by numbering off 1-2, 1-2, 1-2, and so on. Inner and outer circles are created with the "2s" forming a circle around the "1s." Each group is seated on chairs. The "2s" align themselves so that they are seated directly across from the person they are going to observe. Each "2" observes a different "1" and no "1" is to be observed by more than one "2."

The "1s" receive the following topic to reflect upon while the "2s" receive their directions—Topic A: *Which men and women, alive in the world today, do you most admire and appreciate?*

While the "1s" are thinking about the person they admire most, the "2s" are informed they are to observe the person they have chosen in the inner circle. Specifically, they are to become aware of (a) what they see going on within the inner circle, (b) what they hear taking place, and (c) how they *feel* about what they saw and heard taking place. The "2s" observe while the "1s" share their position on the topic identified above. Only the "1s" verbally participate on this topic. The "2s" are restricted to observation.

The "1s" receive 15 minutes during which each person may verbalize their position on the selected topic. The "1s" are not to discuss the topic. Each person merely shares his or her position on the topic without running the risk of having to defend a choice.

After 15 minutes have elapsed, the "2s" get together with the person they observed and give this person feedback based on what was seen, heard, and felt. Upon completion of this procedure, the "1s" and "2s" reverse positions and a new topic is selected: Topic B—*Concerning the times we are living in, to what degree are you inclined to be optimistic in your outlook toward life? Why?*

Faith No. 2—How's it going? A personal assessment. The facilitator uses a random process to pair the participants. They are invited to reflect upon four topics:

1. In these times of changing lifestyles, how does it feel to be a member of your sex?
2. How is it going in your relationships with the significant others in your life?
3. How is it going in your job or school?
4. What reasons do you have for being optimistic about your future?

After the participants have used several minutes to reflect upon the above, the facilitator seeks a volunteer from each pair. The volunteer is the listener while the other person takes the next 4 minutes and shares as much as is desired on the above topics. The person sharing does all of the talking while the volunteer listens.

After 4 minutes have elapsed, the person listening takes 2 minutes and provides feedback. Then the process is reversed.

After the process is completed, the facilitator invites the group to form a circle. Then the participants are provided an opportunity to share what they noticed, found surprising, or discovered.

Faith No. 3—Stepping stones. The facilitator invites the participants to pair up and reflect upon the following:

- As a student, what has been said to you regarding your performance that was encouraging?
- In your life, of which accomplishments are you most proud? Which abilities did you demonstrate in each of these accomplishments?

After sufficient time for reflection, the facilitator invites a volunteer in each pair to begin sharing responses to the above questions. Four minutes are provided for sharing and 2 minutes for feedback. Then the process is reversed. The activity is debriefed with the sharing of awareness and insights.

Faith No. 4—Exploring fundamental philosophical questions. (The following supplies are needed: paper and pencils.) The participants are invited to number off and form small groups of three persons. Within each small group of three persons, someone is designated as "A," another as "B," and a third as "C."

"A" begins by asking "B" one of the questions that follow. "C" functions as a recorder, noting "B's" responses to "A's" question. "A" *active listens* to "B's" responses and repeats the question until 3 minutes have expired. "C" gives "B" the written record of her responses. Then each person shares what he or she became aware of, noticed, or found surprising. The roles are switched until each person has performed in all three capacities.

Questions:

1. What is the nature of human nature?
2. What is the origin of inequality in humanity? Was it authorized by natural law?
3. In which ways and to what degree does society discriminate against your natural self?
4. What constitutes the ideal relationship between the individual and the state?
5. In a democracy, what is the source of the "rights and responsibilities" of both the citizen and the state?
6. Where is true happiness to be found?
7. Should your education fit you more for society or for the full development of your potential?
8. Of all human passions, which are most natural and which are least natural to humanity?

Stage 6: Responsibility

Responsibility Is the Precondition to Purposefulness

Schools and other institutions in our society frequently deny young people the opportunity to assume appropriate levels of responsibility. This causes students to become more dependent and typically to look to others for direction. Each of us has the capacity to effectively manage our own life and it is appropriate for us to gradually assume this responsibility as we mature. The following activities are designed to cultivate self-responsibility.

Responsibility No. 1—Could it be . . .? (The following supplies are needed: labels with preassigned three-digit numbers, related in a logical manner to three or four other numbers—that is, 306, 324, 333, and 360 are numbers with digits that add up to 9, or 205, 223, 232, and 250 are digits adding up to 7—one number per label.) A label is placed on each participants' back. No one should become aware of his or her number prior to the commencement of this activity. The participants are invited to ascertain the specific number recorded on their label by asking only three questions:

1. "Is it higher than . . . ?"
2. "Is it lower than . . . ?"
3. "Could it be . . . ?"

The participants mill about the room asking as many persons as they wish using the above three questions. When they have uncovered the correct number, they may sit down.

When it appears that most of the participants have completed this portion, they are invited to group themselves together with the other persons whose numbers are of a related nature (all the 300s get together, all the 400s, and so on). Then they begin to process awareness, discoveries, surprises, and things they may have noticed while they were attempting to determine their numbers.

While processing awareness, the participants are invited to look for patterns that may reside in the numbers that members in their group received. (Therefore, it is necessary for the facilitator to have given some forethought to choosing numbers that fit certain patterns.) Then the participants report the various patterns they uncovered to the group at large.

The activity is completed with the facilitator processing awareness and insight uncovered by the participants.

Responsibility No. 2—The Pony Sale. (The following supplies are needed: chalkboard or newsprint and markers.) The facilitator invites the participants to relax and listen carefully to a story. The story follows:

Rosalia had a pony given to her by her father, Tony D'Angelo. One day D'Angelo looked out the window and saw Rosalia's pony and decided to sell the pony to his neighbor, Luis Lopez. D'Angelo took Rosalia's pony over to Lopez's home and told him: "Luis, I have the perfect gift for your son, Romero. I'll sell you this pony for $60." Luis thought about D'Angelo's offer and decided to buy the pony.

D'Angelo returned home and explained to his wife, Maria, how he had just sold Rosalia's pony to Luis Lopez. Maria responded: "You what? You sold our little Rosalia's pony without even talking it over with her? That was wrong. You've got to get that pony back before Rosalia comes home from school!"

D'Angelo's conscience was pricked and he went immediately to get Rosalia's pony back. He explained his dilemma to Lopez, who listened thoughtfully and finally agreed to sell him the pony but—for $70. D'Angelo argued for the original selling price, but after repeated protestations, agreed to give Luis Lopez the $70 he demanded and started home with Rosalia's pony.

Lopez entered his house and told his wife, Lucia, how he had just picked up a quick $10 from their neighbor, D'Angelo. Upon which Lucia informed Luis that their son Romero was on his way home from school anticipating a pony because she had already called to tell him about the pony. Now Luis realized he had a problem and he dashed out the door to catch up with D'Angelo.

Luis reached D'Angelo just as he entered his yard and explained his problem. D'Angelo, still smarting from the loss he'd taken, agreed to resell the pony to Lopez, but for $80. Luis protested but to no avail and ended up giving D'Angelo the $80. At this point, D'Angelo looked up and saw Rosalia standing in the doorway. In an instant he was overwhelmed with compassion and ran after Luis Lopez, holding out the $80 and demanding the return of the pony. Luis demonstrated a willingness to return Rosalia's pony, but indicated it would take a non-negotiable price of $90. D'Angelo realized he was trapped and gave Luis Lopez the $90 and took back Rosalia's pony.

This completes the story. The participants are to consider if anyone made a profit and, if so, who and how much. The responses are recorded on the chalkboard. The facilitator designates locations in the room for the various answers and invites the participants to stand with the group that they think has the right answer. Using only verbal reasoning (no pencils and paper), the participants reason among themselves and identify who has the best logic for the answer they came up with. Then each group is invited to see if they can convince the participants in the other groups to switch to their position.

The activity is completed with the facilitator inviting the participants to form a circle and to share with the group anything of which they became aware during their participation in this activity. [Correct answer: Lopez—$20.00.] (Adapted from James P. Carnevale, 1971, reprinted with permission.)

Responsibility No. 3—The Transcendental Problem-Solving Process. (The following supplies are needed: paper and pencils.) With few exceptions, our problems are social. Getting along with ourselves and others has never been easy, to which history can well attest. A major obstacle to the resolution of conflict is our tendency to see only one polar position (black/white, either/or, and so on). Receptivity to only considering two alternatives limits people. Such a dichotomy (either/or) usually results in private and public unresolved differences. This narrow understanding has resulted in outrageous violence perpetrated by human beings on human beings. Normal people have killed perhaps 100,000,000 of their kind in the last 50 years alone.

What a waste of human life results when leaders are unable to think beyond steps 1 and 2 (either = 1, or = 2; this = 1, that = 2). We need to educate people to the reality that there are always more than two sides to every issue or conflict.

In an elementary school in rural Japan, Paul Reps (1967) found a method for facilitating awareness that all problems have four sides and a middle. Consider the following examples:

A. **Cultural prejudice**
   Side 1. The Asian culture surpasses the Latino culture.
   Side 2. The Latino culture surpasses the Asian culture.

Side 3. Sometimes the Asian culture surpasses the Latino. Sometimes the Latino culture surpasses the Asian.

Side 4. Neither culture surpasses the other.

Middle 5. Each culture is fully affirmed by me.

B. Feelings and the mind

Side 1. The mind is superior to feelings.

Side 2. Feelings are superior to the mind.

Step 3. Sometimes the mind is superior. Sometimes feelings are superior.

Side 4. Neither is superior. Neither is inferior.

Middle 5. Both are affirmed in me.

C. Bravery and cowardice

Side 1. Here I am brave.

Side 2. Here I am a coward.

Side 3. Here I am both brave and a coward.

Side 4. Here I am neither brave nor a coward.

Middle 5. Both are affirmed in me.

D. A child experiencing difficulty in school

Side 1. I think slowly and poorly in school.

Side 2. I can think quickly and easily when playing at home.

Side 3. Sometimes I think slowly at home. Sometimes I think quickly at home.

Side 4. When I watch TV, I think neither slowly nor quickly.

Middle 5. I can choose when I will think slowly and poorly and when I will think quickly and easily. Both are my responsibility.

E. Pragmatism and idealism

Side 1. Here I am a pragmatist.

Side 2. Here I am an idealist.

Side 3. Here I am both pragmatist and idealist.

Side 4. Here I am neither.

Middle 5. Both are gloriously affirmed in me.

All kinds of subjects and difficulties can be considered in this consciousness-raising approach: (a) to purchase or not to purchase, (b) to participate or not participate, (c) beauty and ugliness, (d) grief and joy—and so on.

The Japanese teacher, Susumu Ijiri (Reps, 1967), who developed this approach finds it is used most effectively when children sit in front of a small pillow. When lying on the floor, a pillow has four sides and a middle. Problems have four sides and a middle. As the child progresses through the steps of the issue/problem, he places his hand symbolically at the four sides of the pillow for each of the first four steps and then cups his hands over the middle of the pillow while verbalizing step 5.

Ijiri describes the activity in the following way. "The center of the pillow (we first used a small rug) represents our originative harmony from which changing conditions stem." He continues, "I may say this but the children feel, experience, and apply it. Looking for difficulties to resolve should help them in many ways as they grow older. It has helped us who are older. We try not to place ourselves in a dominant assertive 1 position but rather to let, we don't know, 1, turn into something we do know, 2" (Reps, P. [1967]. Pillow Education in Rual Japan. *Square Sun, Square Moon.* Toyko, Japan: Charles E. Tuttle Co., Inc. Reprinted with permission).

Teachers using this approach will help children discover their potential for uncovering creative solutions to their problems. Perhaps even more important, children can free themselves from stigmas such as being considered physically unattractive or dumb or inferior. And, when used as a group process approach, the entire class is afforded insight and opportunities for better understanding their classmates as they address issues/problems.

What a different world this would be if our leaders could get together and resolve issues of conflict in this manner. It could happen someday if future leaders were to experience this process in school.

Activity: The facilitator invites the participants to sit in a circle and contemplate various situations in which they could apply the Transcendental Problem-Solving Process. After sufficient time to have identified an issue, the facilitator invites the participants to record on paper the options they have at each of the "five steps."

Upon completion of the five steps, the facilitator invites a volunteer to share what he or she noticed or discovered. Then the facilitator invites the group to share their discoveries.

The activity continues in like manner until all who desire have shared their application of the process. The activity is completed by processing awareness.

Responsibility No. 4—Acting out your citizenship. The facilitator invites the participants to identify the following:

- What are your dominant strengths, talents, and abilities?
- Which of these do you intuitively feel you are meant to do more with?
- Of what benefit are your talents to society? How should you act out your citizenship?

The participants are paired up and invited to share what they desire on the above. After 5 minutes have elapsed, their partner provides feedback. Then the process is reversed, followed by the processing of awareness.

One of the requirements for successful group participation is that each person must come to take responsibility for his or her own actions.

This leads to an actualizing orientation and makes it possible for students to understand the progression from dependence to independence to purposeful living.

We become truly free when we learn to live purposefully. But this freedom must not be confused with capriciousness. It must be interpreted in terms of responsibleness. Therefore, self-responsibility is the precondition to purposefulness.

Stage 7: Purposefulness

Purposefulness Is the Precondition to Courageous and Worthwhile Acts

Intentional or *purposive living* in its simplest terms refers to the phenomenon of choice. The following activities allow the participants to experience choices pertaining to structuring a meaningful life.

Purposefulness No. 1—Consensus Writing. The participants are invited to form small groups of three to five persons through a random process. (The following supplies are needed: pencils and worksheet [Figure 3.11].) Someone volunteers to read the paragraph found on the worksheet. The worksheet contains the first paragraph found in a well-known book. Another volunteer serves as a recorder. After the paragraph has been read, the group is responsible for completing answers to the questions found on the worksheet.

The responses agreed upon by the group are to be reached through consensus (everyone has input and agrees with what is recorded). After the answers have been written down by the recorder, the small groups present their work to the large group. The activity is completed with the facilitator processing awareness, discoveries, surprises, and so on. The book is Harper Lee's (1960) *To Kill a Mockingbird.*

Purposefulness No. 2—Character Education. *Introduction:* Throughout history, certain individuals have distinguished themselves and given glimpses of what we are capable of becoming and doing. Abraham Maslow was among the first to promote the study of such human beings, whom he identified as *self-actualizing* persons. Maslow was convinced psychologists had made a grave mistake by focusing their attention upon average and deviant human beings and then drawing conclusions about normal behavior.

Piero Ferrucci (1990), a graduate in philosophy from the University of Turin, Italy, and a former student and collaborator of Roberto Assagioli,

Consensus Writing

Paragraph 1

"When he was nearly thirteen, my brother Jem got his arm badly broken at the elbow. When it healed, and Jem's fears of never being able to play football were assuaged he was seldom self-conscious about his injury. His left arm was somewhat shorter than his right; when he stood or walked, the back of his hand was at right angles to his body, his thumb parallel to his thigh. He couldn't have cared less, so long as he could pass and punt."

Consensus Writing Recorder's Sheet

1. Who is the author?

2. What is the title of this book?

3. What is the focal point or moral of the book?

4. As a group, please write the second paragraph of this book.

Figure 3.11.
SOURCE: Andersen. *Courageous Teaching*. © 1995. Reprinted with permission.

has pursued Maslow's contention with an examination of excellence in 10 fields of human endeavor. In his book *Inevitable Grace: Breakthroughs in the Lives of Great Men and Women: Guides to Your Self-Realization* (1990), Ferrucci presents a groundbreaking synthesis that offers fresh insights for anyone interested in the expression of human greatness.

Dr. Ferrucci studied the most significant and beautiful experiences in the lives of 500 great men and women of various times and cultures—sages, artists, scientists, mystics, educators, pioneers, philanthropists, political leaders, actors, dancers, and athletes. He discusses in detail their exceptional abilities and transpersonal phenomena. He was particularly interested in uncovering answers to the following questions: (a) What can we learn from these exceptional people that we might apply in our own lives? (b) How did these individuals become capable of such feats? (c) What are the highest expressions of human nature? (d) What were these individuals' moments of greatest happiness? (e) Is there an interconnectedness between these exceptional persons that transcends cultural difference?

Ferrucci shows that transpersonal experiences, rather than being the condition of a few exceptional individuals, are our common heritage and the truest expression of our being. He found that these natural, simple states are within the reach of us all.

Activity: The facilitator provides the participants with an overview of Ferrucci's theory. The participants are then paired by chance. Using the sharing method, each participant responds to the following questions:

1. Which men and which women, in your opinion, offer the best examples of what we should strive for if we are to live a meaningful, quality life?
2. Can an educational system be devised to help young people become better persons? What would be the basic characteristics of such a system?
3. What would be the essential books and courses in such a system?

Purposefulness No. 3—The Microlab. *Focus on Moral Development:* The facilitator invites the participants to divide into two separate groups. This may be accomplished by numbering off 1-2, 1-2, 1-2, and so on.

The "1s" form a circle with the "2s" forming a circle around the "1s." Both groups may sit down. The "2s" align themselves directly opposite one of the "1s." Each "2" indicates the person he or she has chosen so that all are chosen and no one is missed. (See Figure 3.12.)

The "1s" receive a topic (see the topics that follow). While the "1s" are thinking about their topic, the "2s" are informed they are to observe the person they have chosen in the inner circle and to become aware of (a) what they see, (b) what they hear, and (c) how they feel about what they have seen and heard from the person they are observing. The "2s" observe while the "1s" share their position on the topic. The only person the "2s" are to observe is the person they have selected. Only the inner

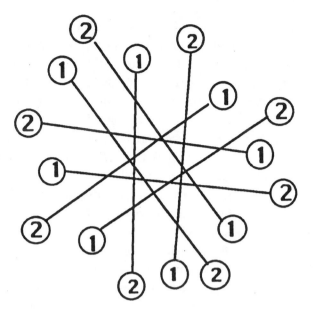

Figure 3.12. Inner-Outer Circle Seating Arrangement

circle verbally participates in this activity. The outer circle is restricted to observing.

The "1s" receive 10 minutes during which they may verbalize their position on the selected topic. The "1s" are not to discuss their topic but to share their personal position on the topic.

After the 10 minutes have elapsed, the "2s" get together with the person whom they were observing and give this person feedback based upon what they have seen, heard, and feel. When this has been completed, the "1s" reverse positions with the "2s" and a new topic is selected.

Topics:

1. If you were to explain what morality means to you, how would you define it?

2. Who, in your opinion, are the most moral men and women (reaching the highest stage of moral development) in the world?

3. What is your attitude toward life? What significance, value, and purpose has life for you? Are you inclined to be optimistic or pessimistic? Why?

4. What do you think about the present political and economic conditions in the world?

5. How is it possible to arrive at a real and lasting peace among the peoples of the world?

6. What is your attitude toward moral principles and demands? Which ideas and feelings do you connect with duty?

7. Do you believe that we are actually at the end of an epoch and at the beginning of a new one? What, in your opinion, are the signs of this renewal? What

characteristics (spiritual, cultural, social, practical) will the new epoch eventually have? (Adapted from Assagioli, R. [1965] *Psychosynthesis*. New York: Sterling Lord Literistic. Copyright © 1965 by Robert Assagioli. Reprinted by permission of Sterling Lord Literistic, Inc.)

Purposefulness No. 4—The Great American Idea. An excellent resource for deepening student understanding on this activity is Garry Wills's (1992) *Lincoln at Gettysburg: The Words That Remade America*. (The following supplies are needed: paper, pencils, and the worksheet [Figure 3.13].) The facilitator distributes the worksheet to the participants and invites a volunteer to read the opening lines to the Declaration of Independence and the Gettysburg Address. After the reading is completed, the facilitator invites the participants to reflect upon the meaning of these two documents and to write a brief essay that addresses the following:

1. What is their significance for the course of history?
2. What meaning do they hold personally for the participants?
3. Are there other documents of comparable significance?

After sufficient time for the students to write their essays, the facilitator randomly divides the participants into small groups of four individuals. Within the small group, the students receive an opportunity to read their essays and to share their perceptions with one another.

The students are reconvened in the large group and invited to reflect upon new insights and changes in their perception from participation in this activity.

Purposefulness No. 5—Personal Insignia. The facilitator provides each participant with a sheet of paper on which a "personal emblem" may be drawn and divided into six compartments. (The following supplies are needed: paper and pencils.) The participants are invited to reflect upon their lives through the examination of six questions. Using their "personal crest," the participants may draw something that symbolizes the essence of what is important to them as a response to each of the following questions:

1. What is your greatest need?
2. What is your dominant personality trait?
3. What is your favorite activity?
4. What is most pleasing to your eyes—most beautiful?
5. What is your greatest source of happiness?
6. What contribution to humanity do you hope to make?

The Declaration of Independence and the Gettysburg Address
A DECLARATION BY THE REPRESENTATIVES OF THE UNITED STATES OF AMERICA, IN [GENERAL] CONGRESS ASSEMBLED

When in the course of human events, it becomes necessary for one people to dissolve the political bands which have connected them with another, and to assume among the powers of the earth, the separate and equal station to which the Laws of Nature and of Nature's God entitle them, a decent respect to the opinions of mankind requires that they should declare the causes which impel them to the separation.

We hold these truths to be self-evident: that all men are created equal; that they are endowed by their Creator with [inherent and] certain inalienable rights; that among these are life, liberty, and the pursuit of happiness . . . (Mayo, 1942, pp. 64-65)

LINCOLN'S GETTYSBURG ADDRESS

Four score and seven years ago our fathers brought forth on this continent a new nation, conceived in liberty, and dedicated to the proposition that all men are created equal.

Now we are engaged in a great civil war, testing whether that nation, or any nation so conceived and so dedicated, can long endure. We are met on a great battlefield of that war. We have come to dedicate a portion of that field as a final resting place for those who here gave their lives that that nation might live. It is altogether fitting and proper that we should do this.

But, in a larger sense, we cannot dedicate—we cannot consecrate—we cannot hallow—this ground. The brave men, living and dead, who struggled here, have consecrated it far above our poor power to add or detract. The world will little note nor long remember what we say here, but it can never forget what they did here. It is for us, the living, rather, to be dedicated here to the unfinished work for which they who fought here have thus far so nobly advanced. It is rather for us to be dedicated to the great task remaining before us—that from these honored dead we take increased devotion to that cause for which they gave the last full measure of devotion; that we here highly resolve—that these dead shall not have died in vain—that this nation under God, shall have a new birth of freedom—and that government of the people, by the people, for the people, shall not perish from the earth. (Wills, 1992, p. 263)

Figure 3.13.

When the participants have completed their drawings, the facilitator invites the group to walk around the room examining each other's personal crest. Then the participants are reconvened in a circle and provided an opportunity to share discoveries, insights, and awareness.

Purposefulness No. 6—A Credo. *New Insight for Purposeful Living.* The facilitator invites the participants to pair up with another person and to reflect upon three questions (The following supplies are needed: paper and pencils.) :

- What is worth knowing?
- What is worth doing?
- What is worth becoming?

Following sufficient time for reflection, the participants take turns sharing and active listening to one another. This is followed with the participants writing a brief essay on how their thinking has changed or evolved while participating in these activities. What is new or different in their thinking? How do they want to live their lives?

The group is reconvened in a circle and each participant receives an opportunity to read his or her essay to the group. The facilitator concludes the activity by processing awareness and meaningful discovery.

Stage 7 activities assist the participants with attaining direction and purpose in their lives. In essence, they ask the participants: "What have been your intentions and what do you want now?" They are a way of integrating past, present, and future in terms of meaningful living. The learning process becomes one of reordering; upon reflection, you can restructure your view of yourself and your understanding and experience of others and the world. Furthermore, you are given deeper insight into intentional living through accepting self-responsibility for determining what is worth knowing, what kind of person is worth becoming, and which activities are worth doing.

Summary

No one can write a generic curriculum of activities for all occasions, levels, subject areas, and so on. No curriculum or program is a panacea for all. However, this presentation of sequenced and developmental activities can provide insight and direction to educators seriously interested in developing their own curriculum. The conceptual framework is readily adaptable to any setting and age group. The practitioner can flesh out this framework with content that is appropriate for any group. The ideal approach is to infuse the process directly into the curriculum so that students experience every lesson as direct participants—sharing and then reflecting upon their new awareness and understanding.

Bibliography

Achievement Motivation Program. (1971). W. Clement & Jessie V. Stone Foundation. Chicago: Combined Motivation Education systems, Inc.

Andersen, J. L. (1977). *A self-development counseling model for schools.* Unpublished doctoral dissertation, Fielding Institute, Santa Barbara, CA.

Andersen, J. L. (1978). *Heartland Area Education Agency human relations: An experiential approach* (Human relations curriculum). Johnston, IA: Heartland Area Education Agency.

Andersen, J. L. (1994). *Classrooms as caring communities* (Human relations curriculum). Johnston, IA: Heartland Area Education Agency.

Assagioli, R. (1965). *Psychosynthesis.* New York: Viking.

Assagioli, R. (1973). *The act of will.* Baltimore: Penguin.

Carnevale, J. P. [San Diego State University]. (1971, October). [Workshops and conversations with author, Algona, IA].

Cornish, E. (1992, November-December). Outlook '93. *The Futurist*, pp. 1-8.

Dreikurs, R. (1953). *Fundamentals of Adlerian psychology.* Chicago: Alfred Adler Institute.

Dreikurs, R. (1957). *Psychology in the classroom* (2nd ed.). New York: Harper & Row.

Dreikurs, R., & Grey, L. (1968). *A new approach to discipline: Logical consequences.* New York: Hawthorn.

Ferrucci, P. (1990). *Inevitable grace: Breakthroughs in the lives of great men and women:Guides to your self-realization.* Los Angeles: Jeremy P. Tarcher.

Frankl, V. (1963). *Man's search for meaning: An introduction to logotherapy.* Boston: Beacon.

Frankl, V. (1969). *The will to meaning.* New York: Plume/New American Library.

Hall, L. (1972, February). *Achievement Motivation Program.* [Workshops and conversations with author, Chicago].

Hesse, H. (1971). *Narcissus and Goldmund.* New York: Bantam.

Hudson, F. M. (1977, October). [Workshops and conversations with author, Santa Barbara, CA].

Jourard, S. (1971). *The transparent self* (2nd ed.). New York: D. Van Nostrand.

Kull, S. (1977). The evening review. *Synthesis 1: The Realization of Self, 1,* 103-107.

Laing, R. D. (1967). *The politics of experience.* New York: Pantheon.

Lee, H. (1960). *To kill a mockingbird.* Philadelphia: Lippincott.

Lewis, H. (1990). *A question of values.* New York: Harper & Row.

Lowen, A. (1972). *Depression and the body.* Baltimore: Pelican.

Lowen, A. (1975). *Bioenergetics.* New York: Coward, McCann & Geoghegan.

Maslow, A. (1954). *Motivation and personality* (2nd ed.). New York: Harper & Row.

Maslow, A. (1970). *Religions, values and peak experiences.* New York: Viking.

Maslow, A. (1971). *The farther reaches of human nature.* New York: Viking.

May, R. (1969). *Love and will.* New York: Norton.

Mayeroff, M. (1971). *On caring.* New York: Harper & Row.

Mayo, B. (1942). *Jefferson himself.* Charlottesville: University Press of Virginia.

Montagu, A. (1950). *On being human.* New York: Hawthorn.

Perls, F. S. (1969). *Gestalt therapy verbatim.* Lafayette: Real People Press.

Postman, N., & Weingartner, C. (1969). *Teaching as a subversive activity.* New York: Delacorte.

Purpel, D. E. (1989). *The moral and spiritual crisis in America.* New York: Bergin & Garvey.

Reps, P. (1967). *Square sun, square moon.* Tokyo, Japan: Charles E. Tuttle Co., Inc.

Rogers, C. R. (1961). *On becoming a person.* Boston: Houghton Mifflin.

Rogers, C. R. (1969). *Freedom to learn.* Columbus, OH: Charles E. Merrill.

Rogers, C. R. (1977). *On personal power: Inner strength and its revolutionary impact.* New York: Delacorte.

Wills, G. (1992). *Lincoln at Gettysburg: The words that remade America.* New York: Simon & Schuster.